THE WAYFARER BOOK

FIFTH EDITION

THE WAYFARER BOOK V Edition

First published in 2010 by The United Kingdom Wayfarer Association
Reprinted 2012

Copyright © 2012 The United Kingdom Wayfarer Association

All rights reserved. No part of this publication may be reproduced, stored in a retrieval system or transmitted, in any form or by any means, electronic, mechanical, photocopying, recording or otherwise without the prior written permission of the publishers and copyright holders. While reasonable care has been taken in the preparation of this book, the publisher takes no responsibility for the use of the methods or products described in the book.

ISBN 978-0-9564671-0-2

Graphic design, compilation and editing by Ray Scragg MBCS CITP
Printed and bound by Impress Print, Corby

ACKNOWLEDGEMENTS

The source materials were based on the Fourth Edition of 2002 whose authors were Ralph Roberts, Martin Collen Snr., Simon Winn, Michael McNamara, Ian Porter, Stuart Rix, Earl Schnur, Paul Wren and Simon Townsend and which was compiled and edited by Elizabeth Reed.

The Executive Committee of the United Kingdom Wayfarer Association would like to thank the following for providing additional source materials for the Fifth Edition: Al Schonborn and Michael McNamara via the Wayfarer Institute of Technology website, Ralph Roberts, Quentin Strauss, Bob Harland, Matt Sharman, David Williams, Anne and Dennis Kell, John and Olwen Mellor, Cath Longhurst and Tracey Newman.

PHOTOGRAPHIC CREDITS

Copyright rests with the individuals listed below:
The Proctor Family: Forward Page, P1L; Nick Richards P1R; Frank & Margaret Dye: Inside back cover, P64
David Harding www.sailingscenes.co.uk: Outside cover, title page, P5, 15, 16, 22, 25, 26, 29, 32
Jesper Nothlev & Soeren Svarre: Contents page right, P8, 18, 23, 30, 31, 48, 82
Jelle Feenstra: Contents page middle, P34; Ken Jensen: Contents page 2nd from left
Al Schonborn: Contents page 4th from left, P54; Jeremy Evans: P20
Brian & Maria Whitmey: P27; Dave Barker P52, 74; David Williams: P56; Sten Willstrand: P58
Dennis & Anne Kell: P65R; Charles Ferrar: P65L; John Mellor: P62; Bob Harland: P64, 76
Arthur Leigh: P69; Ralph Roberts: P70, 71; Chris Codling: P72
Mike Playle: P63; Philippa Helyar: P78, 80; Monica Schaefer: P83

CONTACTS

CONTACT DETAILS CAN BE FOUND ON THE FOLLOWING WEBSITES:

United Kingdom Wayfarer Association	www.wayfarer.org.uk
Canadian Wayfarer Association	www.wayfarer-canada.org
Netherlands Wayfarer Association	www.wayfarer.nl
Scandinavian Wayfarer Association	www.wayfarer.dk
United States Wayfarer Association	www.uswayfarer.org
Wayfarer International Committee	www.wayfarer-international.org
Wayfarer Copyright Holder and Builder	www.hartleyboats.com (Hartley Boats)

PREFACE

The pressure was growing – Sarah, the UK Wayfarer Association Secretary was being inundated with requests for a copy of the Wayfarer Book - but it was out of print. What to do? Ralph Roberts got the ball rolling by breathing on the text of the previous 4th edition of 2002. This process was aided by Quentin Strauss, who updated the references to the Racing Rules of Sailing and produced a new section on 'Winning the Start' too. Looking at the diagrams it was evident that things had changed – bridles had replaced travellers, cascade kickers had replaced levers, cascade jib tensioners had replaced muscle boxes. How about slot gaskets and mast rams? The previous text and graphics had done sterling work but this was beginning to look like a major revision. Oh, and by the way we have a shiny new Mark IV Wayfarer too! So the opportunity for a fresh edition was taken, building in all this new material at the same time.

The first chapter introduces all the Wayfarer types, key components and rigging, up to and including how to step the mast properly – the latter being on the basis that correct mast set-up isn't only for racers! The second chapter starts to get to the nitty-gritty of sail control - essential for racers, but beneficial to a cruiser's understanding of how to get the best out of the rig. Spinnaker handling has been expanded on; I have shamelessly raided material from the Wayfarer Institute of Technology website and am indebted to Al Schonborn and Michael McNamara for its use. The presence on the Mark IV of a spinnaker chute, first introduced on the Wayfarer World, suggested the need for some notes on how this affects spinnaker hoisting and recovery. Many thanks to Cath Longhurst and Tracey Newman – probably the Wayfarer class's most experienced protagonists with the chute - for coming up trumps with these details.

The third chapter on Race Tactics and Strategy mostly survives unscathed from the previous edition, apart from the racing rules references and more thoughts on starting techniques mentioned above. Many thanks to Michael McNamara again, Quentin Strauss, Ian Porter, Stuart Rix, Simon Townsend and Earl Schnur for the continued use of this material – race strategy seems to be one area which hasn't changed that much!

From racing strategy we make the jump to cruising strategy in Chapter Four. This explores the delights of cruising, with guidelines as to necessary equipment and experience levels. Some of the racing discussions of the previous chapter describe how the ideas presented are brought together into practice; this type of approach seemed to be missing in the previous edition's cruising text. As sources for this, there are hundreds of logs to refer to on-line and in Wayfarer News; but I thought it would be helpful to include a short report from Anne & Dennis Kell, which quite admirably describes a short coastal passage and how issues like time scales and weather affect decision making during a trip. There have also been several logs of trips to the Western Isles of Scotland, which seems to me to be a tantalising area to explore. So I couldn't resist including a short report of one of John Mellor's trips to Jura which demonstrates decision making in action. I thank Anne and Dennis Kell and John Mellor for their insightful contributions. I have also taken the opportunity to showcase one or two of Olwen Mellor's cartoons, which I think hit the nail on the head in the cruising chapter. Olwen has contributed her work to Wayfarer News for many years, so a big vote of thanks from me!

The fifth chapter is the 'Comfort and Safety Zone' and includes references to new personal buoyancy standards, clothing, reefing and capsize drills needed to support our ambitions of the previous two chapters. Again there are elements here for cruisers and racers alike. Special thanks are due to Bob Harland, Matt Sharman and David Williams for their updated source materials on reefing, previously published in Wayfarer News. The final chapter covers the important area of trailing which is often taken for granted but which so facilitates our reach into new areas - both in cruising and racing. This is rounded off with a necessarily brief look at maintenance issues.

It was decided at an early stage to use digital image-based graphics to replace drawings and I hope this works well. Many of the photographs originate from the camera of David Harding (www.sailingscenes.co.uk), who has been extremely generous to the Wayfarer Association over the years; many thanks are due to him. The International Championships in Denmark 2007 were a rich source of perceptive images – if only I had more space – I thank Jesper Nothlev and Soeren Svarre for these. Thanks are due to several other individual contributors of pictures and information - too many to name. Last but not least, I would like to thank Roger Proctor for writing the Foreword.

So what have we got? The book is of course very Wayfarer-specific. It starts off with some basic diagrams but moves rapidly on to a lot of thought-provoking detail. For beginners, the book should be read alongside other general books on sailing, navigation, and weather forecasting. For racers, the Racing Rules of Sailing too - if all the suggestions could be implemented consistently we would no doubt have some new champions! For experienced sailors, the book can be dipped into for valuable tips and reminders. Welcome to the Wayfarer Book V edition!

Ray Scragg, W7698, Bluejay, December 2009

Reprint 2012. The first print run sold more quickly than expected. The opportunity has been taken to revise the reefing section and update a small number of images.

Ray Scragg, W10828, Nutcracker, July 2012

CONTENTS

1. **AN INTRODUCTION TO WAYFARERS**   1

   History • Wayfarer Associations • Wayfarer Marks • Principal Parts
   Centreboard & Rudder • Mast & Boom • Sail Controls • Rigging • Mast Set-up
   Rigging the Spinnaker • The Spinnaker Pole System • Spinnaker Launching and
   Retrieval Methods • The Asymmetric Spinnaker

2. **SAILING FAST AND EFFECTIVELY**   21

   Choice of Boat for Racing • Sail Controls • Setting the Genoa • Setting the Mainsail
   Light Wind Settings • Medium Wind Settings • Strong Wind Settings • Beating -
   Putting it all Together • Keeping her Flat • Fore & Aft Trim • Roll Tacking and Gybing
   Sail Setting Guide • Leeward and Windward Spinnaker Hoisting • Retrieving
   Spinnaker Trimming • Gybing the Spinnaker • Spinnaker Chute Launching &
   Recovery • Putting it all together - the Spinnaker around a Course

3. **RACING TACTICS & STRATEGIES**   33

   Racing Tips from Michael McNamara • Pre-start Warm-up • Starting • Beating
   Boat Speed • Wind Shifts • Going the Right Way • Rounding Marks, Reaching
   Changing Gear • Weather • Protesting • The Run by Ian Porter • Crewing by
   Simon Townsend • Winning the Start by Quentin Strauss • Winning Tips by Stu Rix
   Ways to Lose a Race by Earl Schnur • An Alternative Approach to Spinnaker
   Handling by Cath Longhurst & Tracey Newman

4. **CRUISING GUIDE AND STRATEGIES**   53

   Cruising Areas • Rallies • Experience Levels • Guidelines for Tidal Sailing
   Guidelines for Extended and Open Sea Sailing • Cruising Logs • Checklist Items
   Rowing • Outboards • Towing other Wayfarers • Anchoring • Beach Landing
   Use of Fenders as Boat Rollers • Bridge Shooting • Boat Tents • Cruise to a Blackwater
   Rally by Anne & Dennis Kell • The Sound of Jura - a Three Island Cruise by John Mellor

5.	**THE COMFORT AND SAFETY ZONE**	73

    Personal Buoyancy • Clothing • Capsizing • Mainsail Reefing • Slab v Rolling
    Genoa Reefing and Furling • Balancing the Rig • The 'Dry' Buoyancy Test
    The 'Wet' Buoyancy Test

6.	**TRAILING, CARE AND MAINTENANCE**	83

    Boat Trolleys and Trailers • Road Towing • Boat Covers • Maintenance
    Removing the Centreboard • Wooden Boat Maintenance • GRP Boat Maintenance
    Care of Centreboard, Rudder and Spars • Care of Sails • Care of Rigging
    Self-Bailers • Tips for Buying a Second-hand Wayfarer

TABLES 1, 2, 3.	Genoa, Mainsail and Tension/Chock Setting Guide	14
TABLE 4.	Mast Set-up Guide	88

Full size plates - a snapshot of Wayfarer activity:
Outside cover images and title page: A new day dawns - Wayfarer Mk IVs - Poole Week, Dorset, UK, 2009.
Inside front cover: Rantzausminde Rally, Denmark, 2006. Wayfarers lie comfortably to poles in the negligible Baltic tide.
Inside back cover: Wayfarer W48 "Wanderer" about to leave the outer Hebridian island of Pabbay as Frank & Margaret
Dye begin an overnight passage to St. Kilda fifty miles out in the North Atlantic.
Page 20 Michael McNamara & Simon Townsend showing perfect poise during a gusty Bough Beech 'Finale' Nov. 2008.
Page 32 Brownsea Island sets the backdrop for some close quarter spinnaker work - Poole Week 2004.
Page 52 Comfortably at anchor on the Isle of Eigg in the Hebrides 2008.
Page 72 The Wayfarer Flotilla arrives at the Chant de Marin Festival at Paimpol during the Brittany Rally in August 2009.
Page 82 Playing 'Cat & Mouse' at a light-weather International Championships - Denmark 2007.

Further Wayfarer activity - from left to right: The UK Team at the International Rally Denmark 2007; founder of the Scandinavian Wayfarer Association Ken Jensen boat tenting in Norway; a light weather European Championships in Holland 2006; The Maine USA Rally 2008 leader Dick Harrington at one with Blue Mist; One of the first Mark IVs in the Practice Race at the International Championships Denmark 2007

FOREWORD

It is a great honour to have been asked to write this foreword for the fifth edition of the official Wayfarer Book which provides such a great introduction to the world of Wayfarer sailing. It is easy to write about a wonderful boat that has such a long, proud and distinguished history over the last fifty years. It is even easier because it came from the drawing board of my father. It makes me and my family very, very proud.

But we must remember a boat is nothing without the people who sail it. The people who care, are welcoming, sharing, passionate and are prepared to impart their skills, enthusiasm and amazing, sometimes funny, epic tales. The thing that strikes me day after day about the Wayfarer, is the passion and genuine love people feel for the boat. It almost becomes a living thing when people talk about how they want to nurture, protect, encourage and develop the class in equal measure.

This is a boat that has allowed great people to do great things. They have embarked on epic adventures and faced immense mental and physical challenges. Other Wayfarer sailors have raced at the highest levels. But many tens of thousands have had their first sailing experiences in a Wayfarer and indeed learned to sail in it, so engendering a life-long passion and interest in a fantastic sport. And countless others have just gone sailing, for fun, with their friends and their families.

I had the great privilege of going on the 2009 International Rally in Brittany. Having never been on a rally before, I didn't know quite what to expect. I found that I was surrounded by so many friendly people from all around the world. It reflected what an interesting, diverse and resourceful bunch Wayfarer sailors are.

Sailing a Wayfarer with that intrepid cruiser Ralph Roberts was a lovely experience, he even left me alone in his boat, intentionally! It reminded me what a 'kind' boat the Wayfarer is.
A boat that gives you confidence and the ability to be really 'at one with'. Maybe they are clichés, but they are still true!

The Mark IV is a truly new beginning for the boat. Like all change, it can be challenging at times and difficult to get used to. However the Wayfarer is such a great concept and design that it deserves a great new future. I believe that it is set to sail fair for many years to come.

Finally, and unashamedly, I copy the following from the introduction to the Fourth Edition, some words my father wrote:

'To have conceived and designed the instrument on which this multitude of tunes has been played is naturally a source of happiness to me. I am grateful to all those who have played upon that instrument, and hope that they have had as much pleasure from it, whatever the mood or tempo. Without them there would have been only silence. Now let us listen to them'.

So here is to the Wayfarer! And here is to Wayfarer sailors! Good sailing to you all!

Roger Proctor
Ian Proctor Designs, December 2009

Above right: Ian Proctor: The Wayfarer's designer

Below right: Still racing, still winning. W1 was commissioned on 17th March 1957. Production Wayfarers appeared in 1958.

From the early years of Wayfarer racing - note the original small spinnaker which was eventually superseded by the larger one we use today.

AN INTRODUCTION TO WAYFARERS

History of the Wayfarer

Ian Proctor designed the Wayfarer in 1957 as a teaching, racing and cruising sailing dinghy. The design proved to be an outstanding success in this all-purpose role; no other dinghy has since managed to match and maintain its unique popularity. The basic hull shape and overall weight, which laid the foundations for its renowned combination of speed

and seaworthiness, has been retained as originally designed, whilst the interior has been updated over the years to keep pace with user needs and advancing production techniques. A brief description of the various marks is included below. In 2007 the transfer of the Wayfarer Copyright from the Proctor family to boat builders Hartley Laminates was completed. Phil Morrison, the hugely influential designer of National 12s, Merlin Rockets and the RS series, was immediately brought in to design the Wayfarer Mark IV. The concept of the 'Manufacture Controlled One-design Class' as successfully rendered within the RS class was brought into the Wayfarer class, ensuring that all boats are built from moulds that originate from a single master plug to tight manufacturing tolerances. In fifty years, the Wayfarer Class has successfully negotiated the transition from the original pioneering mahogany and marine ply design concept with suitable tolerances for kit-building to today's highly optimised one-design – still available in racing, cruising and training versions as originally envisaged by Ian Proctor.

DIMENSIONS

Length	4.82m	15' 10"
Beam	1.86m	6' 1"
Minimum hull weight	168.7kg	372lb
Draft maximum	1.17m	3' 10"
Draft minimum	0.23m	8"
Mast length	6.88m	22' 7"
Mainsail	8.8 sq m	95 sq ft
Genoa	4.3 sq m	46 sq ft
Jib	2.8 sq m	30 sq ft
Spinnaker	13.5 sq m	145 sq ft
Asymmetric spinnaker	17 sq m	190 sq ft
Portsmouth Yardstick	1099	

United Kingdom Wayfarer Association

The UK Wayfarer Class Association (UKWA) was formed in 1958 with the aim of supporting the interests and activities of Wayfarer owners. Full membership is available for boat owners and their families. Associate membership is open to any non-Wayfarer owner who has an interest in the Class. The Association represents the interests of the Class and its members, and organises various activities, which include cruise and race training events; a racing programme of Club, Area, National and International Championships; and cruising rallies in different parts of the UK, as well as Europe and North America.

The UKWA has an informative website www.wayfarer.org.uk and also publishes a highly acclaimed magazine, 'Wayfarer News'. Both of these news and information resources keep members informed of current activities and developments, and feature a variety of topical articles with regard to racing, cruising and day sailing activities. Queries on any aspect of Wayfarer sailing can be answered quickly and directly on the UKWA Website forum. The Association also runs an insurance scheme through a broker at very favourable rates. The Association Secretary is available to answer any enquiry – be it about the UKWA; buying a Wayfarer; fitting it out; or on any aspect of Wayfarer sailing in the UK or overseas. The Secretary's details can be found on the Wayfarer website.

Wayfarer International Committee (WIC)

In addition to the UKWA there are currently four other National Wayfarer Class Associations (NCAs) - in Scandinavia, Holland, Canada, and the USA. The website addresses for these Associations can be found at the front of this book. The Wayfarer International Committee was established in 1972 to further the interests of the class throughout the world, and to maintain the one-design principle no matter where the Wayfarer was built or raced. The committee is composed of representatives of each NCA, and its activities are coordinated by an International Secretary. Details of the current WIC Secretary can be found on the Wayfarer International Website. (www.wayfarer-international.org). The WIC is responsible for formalising changes to the International Class Rules, where these have been approved by the National Class Associations. Members of each Association have voting rights on a proportional representation basis, and under its constitution, any amendment to the class rules requires a two-thirds overall majority. The WIC is also responsible for coordinating the International and European Racing Championships, both of which are held every three years at a venue set by one of the National Class Associations, on a rotational basis.

Types of Wayfarer

The original Wayfarer Mark1 was designed to be constructed solely in wood – marine ply and mahogany. The latest version - the Mark IV - is designed specifically for glass reinforced plastic (GRP) moulding. The introduction of GRP allowed for the manufacture of a dinghy that was quicker to build and required less maintenance. There have been a number of variations of the internal layout since the original design. Each modification has been carefully considered and only accepted after being scrutinised by the WIC. This has preserved the one-design principle, allowing all Wayfarers to race together on even terms. It has also helped to maintain the boat's second-hand value. An amazing thing about the Wayfarer is that any hull of any type could be acquired, renovated, and then fitted out with new mast, sails, foils and fittings identically to that of a brand new Mark IV boat. The only exception to this would be the lack of spinnaker chute and transom flaps, which are clearly integral parts of the latest hull design. The various marks of Wayfarer are summarised below. As some of the designs were in production concurrently, the sail number ranges below are just a guide.

Mark I – Wood (The Woody)
1958 to 1994 - sail numbers in the range 1 to 9558
The original wooden Wayfarer was available for construction by both amateur and licensed builders. However, self-build kits were eventually phased out. There are a good number of wooden Wayfarers still being sailed, and second-hand ones are usually available. If an old model is bought with the idea of a major renovation for racing use, such rebuild must be notified to the relevant NCA before work is started. On completion, the boat must be thoroughly examined to check that the work has been carried out as specified. All timber must be replaced with wood of the same size and type, and any work carried out that changes the boat's specification so that it no longer conforms to the class rules, invalidates its authenticity as a Wayfarer. The wooden Wayfarer was very sturdily constructed, a factor demonstrated when Frank Dye encountered gales on his trip to Norway – his book 'Ocean Crossing Wayfarer' has been recently re-published. Again, because of their sound construction, there are still many wooden boats built thirty or more years ago that continue to be cruised or raced competitively. They may require more maintenance than their GRP counterparts – but epoxy coatings and improved paints and varnishes have made this much easier. Many owners feel that it is well worth the extra effort for the pleasing appearance of natural wood. The large hatch covers front and rear need to be carefully maintained to ensure the integrity of the buoyancy compartments.
Cruising Attributes: The bow and stern tanks provide a large volume of protected stowage for gear, though access is limited at the front.

Mark I – GRP
1965 to 1980 - sail numbers in the range 1077 to 4130
This design, introduced in 1965, was the first transition from wood to GRP and is similar in layout to the wooden boat. Over two thousand boats of this type were built, with many still in regular use. Its most distinguishing feature compared with the later Mark II is that the forward buoyancy tank fills most of the area beneath the foredeck. The large hatch covers front and rear need to be carefully maintained to ensure the integrity of the buoyancy compartments.
Cruising Attributes: The bow and stern tanks provide a large volume of protected stowage for gear, though access is limited at the front.

Mark II – GRP
1974 to 2007 - with sail numbers from 3907 onwards
This design included a number of improvements, particularly the front and rear buoyancy tanks being built into the hull before bonding on the deck. Additional strengthening was given to the hull to support the floorboards. The large rear hatch cover needs to be carefully maintained to ensure the integrity of the buoyancy compartment.
Cruising Attributes: A noticeable feature of the Mark II is a shelf between the front buoyancy tank and the foredeck. This provides for easier access when storing items for cruising, though any gear that needs to be kept dry - in the event of a capsize - should be stored in waterproof 'Dri-bags'.

Mark II SD – GRP
1986 to 1994 - with sail numbers from 8280 onwards
Cruising Attributes: The self-draining (SD) design was introduced for the benefit of those owners who kept their boats on moorings, since any water in the boat automatically drained from the two self-bailers on each side of the hull. The sealed area between the floor and the hull raised the floor above the level of the water, which provided an additional volume of buoyancy. This tended to make the boat invert more readily after it had capsized. After righting, water tended to surge from one side of the boat to the other, causing some instability. To help overcome this, drain tubes could be fitted through the stern tanks. The raised floor also gave less room under the thwart for sleeping. The front shelf of the standard Mark II above was retained.

Mark IA – GRP
1987 to 2007 - with sail numbers from 8499 onwards
This version combined all the Mark II improvements in design, with the Mark I concept of having a full under-foredeck bulkhead. The hatch covers front and rear need to be carefully maintained to ensure the integrity of the buoyancy compartments. **Cruising Attributes:** Unlike the Mark I, the bulkhead was divided horizontally into two watertight compartments, each with its own large sealed hatch cover. It was designed to give added storage space for cruising, though access is limited by the mast and tabernacle.

Mark III – GRP
From 1981, with sail numbers from 7579 onwards
This version was built by Abbott Boats in Canada, and is generally found only in North America. The Mark III is no longer in production, after a devastating fire at the builders' works.

Plus S – GRP
1991 to 2007, sail numbers in the range 9022 to 10505
A foam sandwich construction was introduced in 1991, in order to give the hull of the GRP Wayfarer the same degree of stiffness and weight distribution as that of a wooden Wayfarer. The structure of the mast tabernacle was also strengthened. The result was designed to negate any advantage that racing owners of wooden boats might have had over the plastic version. The design of the forward bulkhead reverted from the shelf of the Mark II back to the Mark I concept of having a full depth tank but with only a small inspection hatch providing access - though a larger watertight hatch cover was available as a cruising option. The large rear hatch cover needs to be carefully maintained to ensure the integrity of the buoyancy compartment.

Marks IA, II and Plus S – Composite
As the marks above in GRP but finished with a wooden deck, giving them the outer appearance of a wooden boat with a painted hull.

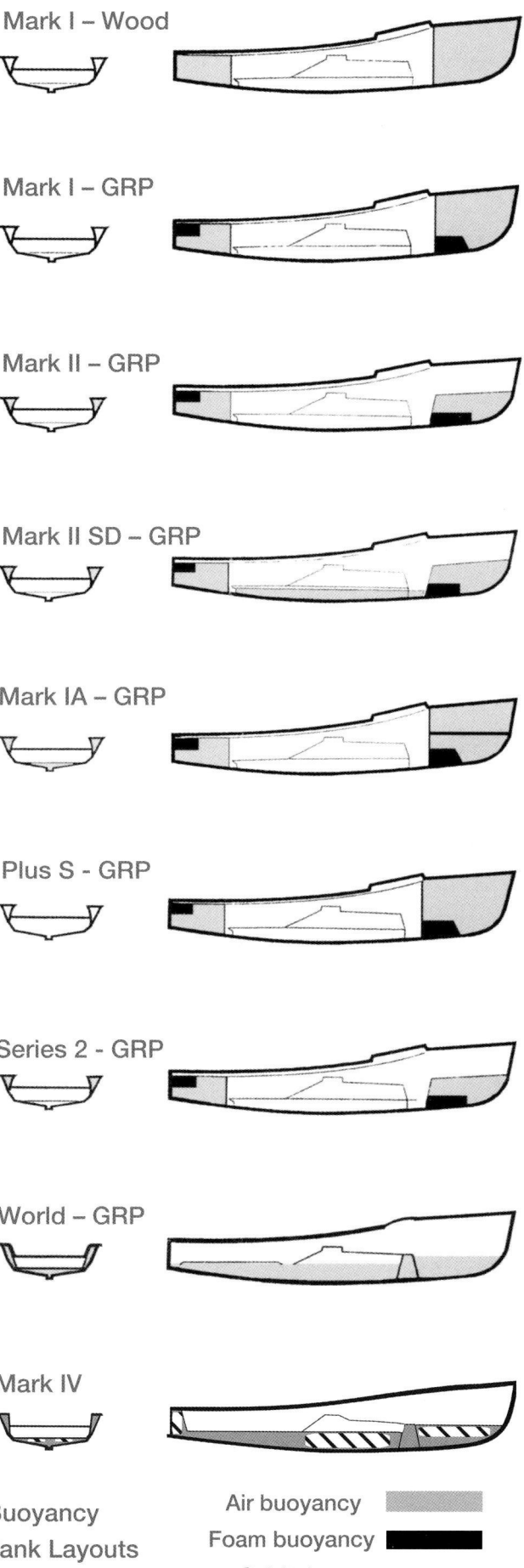

Series 2 – GRP versions
From 1993 to 2007
Series 2 versions of the above designs contained a few minor modifications. They were introduced when the original plugs and moulds needed replacing and the opportunity was taken to make slight improvements to the design for the new moulds.

World – GRP
1997 to 2007 with sail numbers in the range 9821 to 10505
Built entirely of GRP, the Wayfarer World, introduced in 1997, was the most fundamental design change since the original Wayfarer - the internal shape being radically changed to accommodate spinnaker chute, self-draining transom flaps and mid-bilge self-bailers. There are three sealed buoyancy tanks between the inner and outer hull mouldings. An optional asymmetric spinnaker pole system was available though not approved for racing. The self-bailers work very efficiently at removing any excess water whilst sailing.
Cruising Attributes: A raised foredeck and a low under foredeck floor provide considerable stowage for cruising. However the asymmetric spinnaker option considerably reduces the amount of storage space under the foredeck for cruising, particularly the later versions with a swinging bowsprit. This was the first version not to have an integral aft buoyancy/ storage tank, though there is considerable space for removable waterproof storage bags, or containers or a GRP box. There is over 1.8m length of free space available for sleeping when the rear storage is removed.

Wayfarer World Plus S Type – GRP
2002 to 2007 with sail numbers up to 10505
The Wayfarer World +S Type has the same layout as the standard Wayfarer World. However, the hull incorporates a foam sandwich construction giving the increased panel stiffness of the Series 2 Plus S.

Mark IV GRP & Foam Sandwich Options
From 2007 with sail numbers from 10506 onwards
This is the latest Wayfarer version, designed by Phil Morrison. With its flatter foredeck and dished transom it brings the characteristic Morrison look and functionality to the Wayfarer. As with the 'World', the Mark IV is built from three distinct GRP mouldings - buoyancy tank areas being sealed off and separate from stowage areas. However, unlike the World, buoyancy has been reintroduced into the transom area. The side decks are rolled, rather than flat, making it more comfortable for both helm and crew to sit out, and the centre thwart has been brought slightly further aft to provide more space for the crew. As with the 'World' version, the foredeck no longer has the Wayfarer's trademark washboards, but does incorporate a spinnaker chute, as well as an optional asymmetric pole system for non-racing use. The design incorporates self-bailers and transom flaps at the stern, allowing water to drain rapidly after a capsize. There is a training version, a cruising version, and an extra-stiff foam sandwich version for racing. Further information is available from Hartley Laminates, who are the Wayfarer copyright holders and builders – see their website at www.hartleylaminates.co.uk.
Cruising Attributes: Like the World, the Mark IV has potentially large and accessible storage capacity front and rear - space is available to accommodate an optional rear stowage box roomy enough to take a small outboard motor.

Measurement Certificates
A Certificate of Measurement provides evidence that a Wayfarer hull, sails, spars and other ancillary equipment comply with the Class Rules and building specifications. It also includes the buoyancy test log, which needs to be signed off each year. The up-to-date certificate is required to be produced at Wayfarer UKWA Open, Area, National, and WIC International events. Apart from enabling crews to experience competition in events at a higher level than club racing, a measurement certificate can also add value to a second-hand Wayfarer – particularly when being sold as a racing version. A list of class measurers is given on the Wayfarer website and is also available from the Class Association Secretary.

It is possible for UKWA members to check whether a second-hand Wayfarer has a Certificate of Measurement by contacting the Class Secretary who holds the measurement records. If this doesn't exist, it will be necessary for a Class Measurer to carry out a thorough inspection to obtain a valid certificate. There is no fixed fee for this; the cost will depend on the amount of time required which in turn depends on the mark and condition of the boat. It is therefore prudent to carry out a pre-measurement check in order to rectify the most basic faults that might prevent the boat being passed – saving your own and the measurer's time. A copy of the measurement form for each mark of boat, as well as the Class Rules can be found on the WIC website. The key areas for self-check are: the black bands on spars; the foil profiles; the buoyancy tank seals; and the builders licence plate. The Class Measurer examines the boat, and completes a measurement form that itemises the class rules for the particular mark of Wayfarer being measured. All observations during the process are noted on the form. The measurer would normally discuss these with the owner and may well offer advice relating to both the measurement and the boat set-up. If a boat fails to measure because of discrepancies that cannot be easily rectified, the details can be submitted to the Rules and Technical Sub-Committee and a dispensation may be granted in exceptional circumstances. On successful completion, the Association Secretary will issue a certificate to the owner, together with a copy of the measurement form.

Change of ownership and structural changes
A certificate is valid until the boat changes owners, when a replacement certificate should be applied for from the Association Secretary. She will ensure that contact details are updated – re-measurement not being necessary. If structural changes are made, particularly any which affect the boat's weight or shape, the boat will need to be re-measured. The Association is available to assist with any difficulties arising during this process.

The Principal Parts of a Wayfarer

1	Shrouds	12	Gudgeons / pintles	23	Mast Ram (optional)
2	Forestay	13	Lifting rudder blade	24	Mainsail leech
3	Shroud adjusters	14	Chines	25	Genoa Leech
4	Gooseneck	15	Centreboard	26	Genoa Luff
5	Boom	16	Thwart	27	Spinnaker pole
6	Kicking strap (Vang)	17	Spinnaker sheets	28	Transom
7	Bridle	18	Toestraps	29	Foredeck
8	Mainsheet block / jammer	19	Transom flaps	30	Tabernacle
9	Tiller	20	Main sheet	31	Self-bailers
10	Tiller extension	21	Jib sheet	32	Slot gaskets
11	Rudder stock	22	Barber hauler (optional)	33	Keel bands

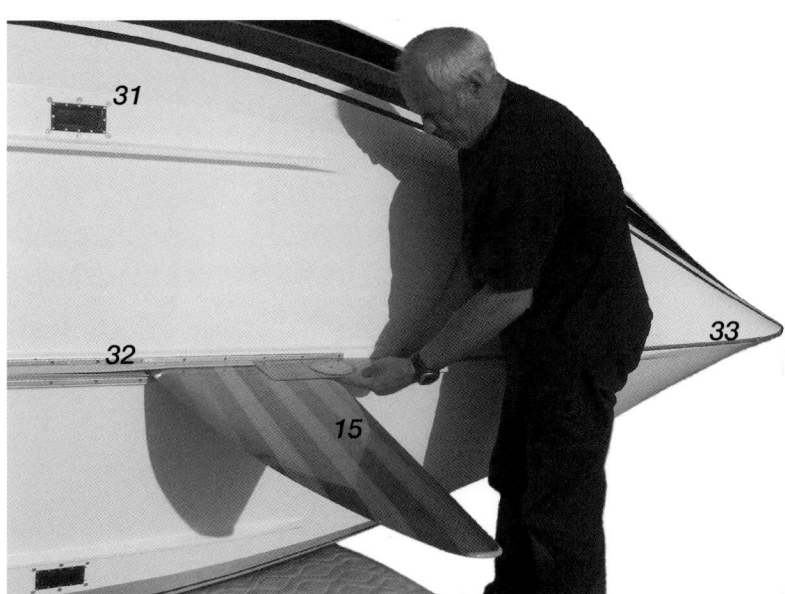

Centreboard

Of GRP, plywood or wood/epoxy construction, the size, shape, thickness and aerofoil section of the centreboard, as well as its position and projection when fitted in the boat, are closely controlled by the class rules. The centreboard must be set up in the boat correctly, as the rig balance depends on its position of resistance to leeway relative to the centre of effort created by the sails. When fully raised, the centreboard must not project below the keel. When fully down, the angle of the leading edge relative to the keel must be no more than 83 degrees, (see left) with the stopper at the top of the centreboard being adjusted to maintain this angle.

At the same time, the centreboard penetration below the keel should be checked – it needs to be a minimum of 965mm and a maximum of 1008mm. There is a centreboard friction grip which can be adjusted by two screws, accessible when the board is fully down, to ensure there is no play at the top of the centreboard case and preventing the board coming up when sailing. It is useful to fit a strap to the stopper to make the centreboard easy to adjust whilst sailing. It is also important that there is no play between the centreboard and the bottom of the centreboard casing - packing strips may be glued to the inner casing surface as necessary. The centreboard pivot bolt is situated below the floor. This bolt, with a locking nut and large metal washers, compresses PVC or nylon washers to prevent the ingress of water. On the Wayfarer World and Mk IV, the pivot bolt is secured between the inner and outer hulls, and cannot be accessed. The centreboard on these models is removed from the boat by unscrewing the retaining clip accessed beneath the centreboard slot on the hull. A brass strip is often incorporated in the leading edge to help prevent it becoming damaged when hitting any object, or grounding when sailing in shallow water.

Although not mandatory, it is considered good practice to fit centreboard slot gaskets. These are strips of folded sailcloth, stretched tightly between the keel-bands and the keel, which close off the centreboard slot. They open up just sufficiently to allow the board through. Two main advantages: firstly, they greatly reduce the turbulence under the boat so enabling a nice smooth wake; it is well established that this increases performance while allowing the rudder to operate more efficiently. Secondly, they provide some protection of the centreboard box from the ingress of sand and pebbles, which can damage or jam the centreboard.

The blade is able to pivot on a bolt through the stock, so that the leading edge can be raised in-line with the bottom of the boat. It is important that there is no side-to-side play between the rudder and stock, in the rudder hangings, or between the tiller and tiller extension. In this respect anodised rudder stocks used with aluminium tillers have proved to be superior to their traditional wooden predecessors. Rudder hangings need to be strong as the forces generated are enormous - check that they are the extruded aluminium types with 8mm pins and that they are through bolted to the transom. Tiller extensions should be about 75mm short of the transom when folded back. The leading edge of the blade should be vertical under way, but can be raised a little in light airs to give a bit more feel.

A length of rope attached to the front of the blade just below the stock together with a cleat on the tiller are used to keep the rudder blade down – the blade must not be allowed to rise inadvertently when sailing. It is important to remember to uncleat the line when approaching shallower water. Auto-release cleats are now available, which release on accidental grounding. A refinement of this is to insert a pulley block to give a two to one purchase to force the rudder blade down – a line, with one end attached to the tiller is passed through the pulley block and back to the cleat. Some people also use a similar piece of rope for a rudder uphaul to keep the blade safely above the ground when ashore or in shallow water. However, this has largely been superseded by the use of a large wing-nut on the swivel bolt, which enables the friction between the blade and the stock to be adjusted.

Rudder Assembly

The rudder assembly consists of the blade, stock and tiller. There are two main rudder blade profiles - the standard blade, and a slightly deeper and straighter blade, which some racing helms prefer, particularly when racing at sea. However, the standard slightly shallower and more rounded profile tends to give a better 'feel' and more immediately transmits any imbalance in trim or sail setting to the helm – this is especially so now that centreboard slot gaskets are permitted. New or replacement blades are usually of GRP or wood/epoxy. If preferred, the rudder blades can be hand made from either 19 or 21mm plywood as long as it is remembered that like the centreboard, the dimensions and aerofoil section are strictly controlled by the class rules. As with the centreboard too, a brass strip, incorporated in the leading edge of the blade, will help to prevent it being damaged when sailing in shallow water.

Left and above: The standard rudder assembly showing down-haul rope and cleat.

Right: The optional long rudder blade

Mast and Boom

Wayfarers originally had masts and booms crafted from spruce. But very few of these spars are seen these days - there are a few enthusiasts who appreciate being able to follow the original design in all respects - drawings are still available. The standard mast specified in the class rules is the Selden section E. This alloy mast is tapered at the top to reduce weight and windage, with the main, genoa, and spinnaker halyards running down inside the mast. Spreaders, sheaves, and shroud fixings have evolved over the years but the basic arrangement of adjustable spreaders with sheaves for main, jib, and spinnaker halyards, and sheaves for spinnaker pole uphaul and downhaul remains unchanged. Strengthening collars at deck level have been a standard fitment for many years. Care needs to be taken when threading the halyards down the mast to ensure they do not become intertwined. The sheaves on the upper parts of the mast, as well as those at the foot, should be checked regularly to ensure they run freely.

A number of boom sections have been used over the years as sail control has become more efficient. The original aluminium boom was pear-shaped with no underside integral track. This was replaced by an oval-shaped boom, with the most recent being the 5-sided Selden 2633 section. This is recommended as being stiffer and lighter than its predecessors, though the original C-section and subsequent 2520 section are still permissible. The later booms have an underside slider track for main and kicker take-offs. It is possible to attach all the various fittings needed for cruising or racing along this underside track, and a purchase system for the mainsail clew outhaul can be installed within the boom. The latest facility to have up to two additional sheaves at each end of the boom could provide more rigging options. Masts and booms are anodised in silver finish, or at additional cost, in black.

Standing Rigging

The mast is supported by two shrouds and a forestay. The length of the wire for the shroud is 4.826m for use with, for example, an Allen shroud adjuster A4272. The wire used is 3mm diameter 1x19 stainless steel. The shroud length governs the rake of the mast, which can be altered by moving the clevis pin position in the shroud adjusters. It is important that the length of each shroud is exactly equal, so that the mast stands evenly in the boat. It is advisable to protect the clevis pin and split ring, by taping it up or covering it with a plastic tube. It is also advisable to make sure the ends of the spreaders are completely smooth so that they will not chafe and damage the mainsail or spinnaker. Newer spreaders have screw-in plastic end fittings that do the job – alternatively the ends can be taped up. It is important for all fittings, particularly the spreaders, to be rigid. The rigging should always be under tension, and the mast braced securely at the foot and at the foredeck, so that the power generated by the sails is directly transmitted to the hull. This is achieved by tightening the genoa halyard, rather than the forestay.

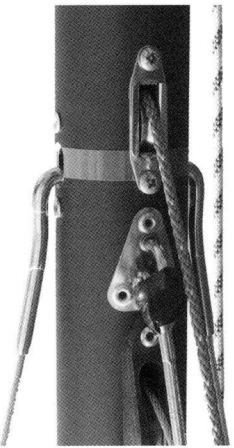

Detail of the mast at the hounds

From top downwards, spinnaker sheave, forestay attachment and jib halyard sheave. The shroud connection tangs are shown each side. The taped measurement band is also seen.

Detail of the mast at the spreaders

Showing the mainsail track and the spreader adjusters

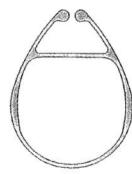

Left: The Selden E section used for masts. Used originally for booms too.

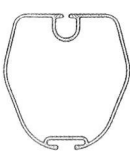 

The 2628 boom section (left) has been superseded by the 2633 section (right).

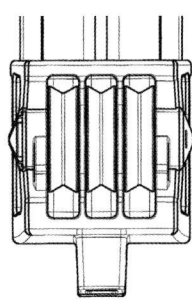 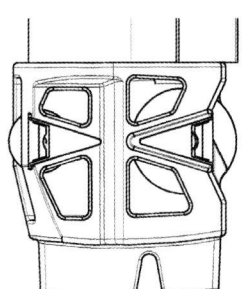

The Selden E section mast heel assembly, has three sheaves at the rear (left) and two sheaves at the front (hidden). Side view (right)

The Sails

The standard sails are a full-sized mainsail, a foresail – which can be the larger genoa or smaller jib, and a symmetric spinnaker for off-wind sailing. There is also an asymmetric spinnaker option for fun sailing and training.

Mainsail

The mainsail is of conventional design with a bolt-roped luff and foot for the mast and boom tracks respectively. The leech areas are stiffened by the use of four battens, the top one being shorter than the bottom three. Where tapered battens are used, the thinner, tapered end is fitted into the batten pocket first. An optional window in the region above the boom aids visibility. Class rules allow an additional upper window in the mainsail to enable the crew to watch a telltale on the leech of the genoa when racing. For cruisers and day sailors, reefing points are an essential addition – and masthead buoyancy should be considered too.

1. *Wayfarer insignia - tail points aft both sides*
2. *Sailhead with stiffening board and cringle*
3. *Foot with bolt rope in boom slot*
4. *Genoa luff with built-in luff wire*
5. *Luff with bolt rope in mast slot*
6. *Window to view genoa leech*
7. *Cunningham cringle*
8. *Clew with cringle*
9. *Tack with cringle*
10. *Sailmaker's logo*
11. *Boat number*
12. *Telltales*
13. *Window*
14. *Battens*
15. *Leech*
16. *Foot*

INTRODUCTION TO WAYFARERS

United Kingdom Wayfarer Association

18 August 2013

Dear Mike

Many thanks for your membership application. On behalf of the Association I should like to offer you a very warm welcome. I hope you will thoroughly enjoy being a member and perhaps join in some of our events.

Please find enclosed a membership sticker, which can be used either on your boat or the outside of your car window, a copy of our current edition of Wayfarer News, our constitution, plus details of our class insurance scheme together with additional, general information. Our re-printed Wayfarer Book is available from me, (see our website for details) plus further information about the Association and our programme of training, cruising and racing events: www.wayfarer.org.uk   Further details / updates for next year will be posted as more information becomes available.

Members are warmly invited to **register for our website,** where there is much, additional information and our extensive cruising log library – which you may find of interest? Members are invited to register for cruising, racing and / or general emails for additional information and updates, between magazines. Your registration has been approved.

Members are also invited to register (separately) for the Members' forum where you can post any queries you may have for other members to answer.

Registered members are welcome to add, edit and subsequently delete their own adverts for any Wayfarer items wanted/for sale, free of charge on our website - and each advert is included in Wayfarer News, too, though without the photos.

Boat owning membership is recorded under boat numbers (not builder's marks). As there was no boat number given in your application, I have given you a temporary Associate membership number **A 1863.** If you are able to tell me your boat number, I will be delighted to update our records accordingly. The boat's number should be found on a small metal plaque fixed somewhere, often on the aft slope of the centreboard case. In the case of a wooden boat it is usually carved on the upstand of the transom. This number is usually, but not necessarily, the same as the number on the sails. If different, it is the boat number I need, not the sail numbers. Membership renewal is due on April 1st each year and a renewal form will sent. New membership applications received after 1 October also cover the following year.

For advice on rules and technical matters the WIC Rules can be found on our website or please contact our R&T Chairman, John Mellor: randt@wayfarer.org.uk

I hope this is helpful. If I can be of any further assistance, please do not hesitate to contact me, and I shall do my best! Good sailing,

Yours sincerely

Sarah Burgess
Secretary

Class Secretary: Sarah Burgess, UKWA, PO Box 10687, Colchester, CO5 8XJ
Tel: 01206 545896 email: secretary@wayfarer.org.uk

Welcome to the Wayfarer Class Association

We pride ourselves on being a very friendly class association and obviously, are always delighted to welcome new members.

UKWA Members

are warmly invited to register for our website

www.wayfarer.org.uk

and sign up for the new, *eNews letters* on either racing / cruising and / or general matters

This is in addition to our full colour, Wayfarer News posted to all members

YOU CAN NOW ENJOY THE BENEFITS OF UKWA MEMBERSHIP which include

- Receiving your own copy of our full colour magazine, Wayfarer News.

- Able to join in our racing, cruising and training events
  Including our annual *Cruising Conference, Cruising rallies, race training* and *National race-circuit*. Our National Champion is invited to compete in the annual Endeavour Trophy along with national champions from other classes.

- Take advantage of our class insurance scheme with Craftinsure

- Hire one of our new boat tents for cruising – the new-design tents, available for the first time last year, are proving extremely popular. To avoid disappointment, please book early – see booking form on our website

- Be able to share the vast amount of knowledge and experience many of our long standing members have, and are only too pleased to share it with newer members to the class.

- Register for our website, with access to our extensive cruising log library and members' forum etc.

- Members can, on registering for the members' only section of our website, sign up for our forthcoming, new, additional *eNews letters* which will be sent out on an ad hoc basis to those who have signed up for them, on racing, cruising and / or general matters. *Sign up – to not miss out!*

- Registered members can add their own adverts for any Wayfarer items wanted/for sale. These adverts are included on both our website and in Wayfarer News.

- Class clothing from Ocean World www.oceanworld.co.uk/wayfarer

- Discounted price for the Wayfarer Book and other items for sale from the Secretary. See our on-line shop, on our website for additional items for sale

- Please encourage your Wayfaring friends / crew to join us: Application forms are available on our website www.wayfarer.org.uk or from the Secretary: secretary@wayfarer.org.uk

They don't have to own a Wayfarer to be a member, and many people choose to join while looking for a boat so that they can take advantage of membership, especially our magazine and website, in the meantime.

Information packs can be sent to anyone who may be interested in joining, which will include our colour brochure, application form, general information on Wayfarers and the UKWA, a back copy of Wayfarer News and a Craftinsure leaflet. Please email secretary@wayfarer.org.uk for one.

Foresails

Foresails guide the wind around the mainsail, increasing the power and efficiency of the rig. The foresail also helps balance the rig and aid manoeuvrability. The two common foresails are the jib and genoa. The genoa is used in light to medium wind conditions, and virtually always when racing; the smaller jib is used in stronger wind conditions, particularly when the mainsail has been reefed. A third foresail has been developed by McNamara Sails, midway in size between a jib and genoa, which combines most of the advantages of the two other sails, and is ideal for family day-sailing, or racing with a younger or less muscular crew in stronger wind conditions. Most standard foresails are made with a wire luff, thus enabling the correct rig tension to be set through the halyard, by means of a highfield lever, muscle box, or cascade system (a combination of pulley blocks). When tensioned, the luff wire of the foresail takes over the role of the forestay, and sets the mast rig tension as well as the entry shape to the foresail. These two factors are vital for good upwind performance; neither being possible with the old method of foresail hoisting in which the foresail had a rope luff, and was attached to the forestay with jib hanks - the forestay providing inadequate rig tension.

Jib/Genoa Sheets and Fairleads

The distance of the genoa fairlead or pulley block in its central position to the outside edge of the transom should be 2380mm and 530mm to the centreline of the boat. The genoa tracks should be positioned so that there is a fore and aft adjustment of up to 75mm either side of this central position. Most genoa tracks are 300mm long, and could be reduced in length if so desired. It is less important for there to be lateral (gunwale to gunwale) adjustment, since easing the genoa sheet to open the 'slot' is far more effective than moving the genoa fairlead position sideways. The genoa sheets should be as thin and light as possible so that they run freely, while allowing the crew to hold them comfortably – between 6mm and 10mm; 8mm is a good starting point. Any good chandler will offer advice as to the most suitable rope to use. It is important for the genoa pulley blocks and cleats to be of the highest possible quality, and always able to release quickly and easily. The jib/genoa sheets can be attached to the sail in a number of ways. Racing helms tend to attach both ends to the sail, running a continuous loop through the boat. This makes it easier for crew and/or helm to find the sheet and avoid entanglements. Cruisers normally have some way of easily attaching the middle of the jib sheet to the foresail, in order to provide for a quick and simple way of attaching or changing the foresails. The two ends may be tied together in the boat if required. Optionally, ratchet blocks may be fitted which take some of the load off the jib sheets in heavier weather.

Optional genoa track assembly with pulley block leading to ratchet block and cam cleat. Also shown is the spinnaker guy cleat (top) and three cam cleats for kicking strap, cunningham, and bridle (or clew outhaul if preferred)

The Kicking Strap

The kicking strap controls the angle of the boom to the mast and therefore the amount of twist in the mainsail. The kicker control system must be sufficiently powerful to achieve the sail control needed to flatten the mainsail in increasing breezes. The minimum purchase required is 6:1, which can be achieved by using two sets of triple blocks, one of which is attached to the boom (usually with a wire strop to reduce the length of the rope required), and the other to the mast foot with a cleat. This can be doubled to 12:1, especially for racing, by having a split control line leading to the helm on both sides of the boat. However, the alternative cascade kicker systems giving at least a 16:1 power ratio have proved popular, as they have the major advantage of freeing off very easily as the wind drops. They can be wire but spliced dyneema is more crew-friendly. Perhaps as a concession to crew comfort, the class rules specify that the kicking strap should not be attached to the boom at a point less than 2109mm from the inner edge of the boom end black band.

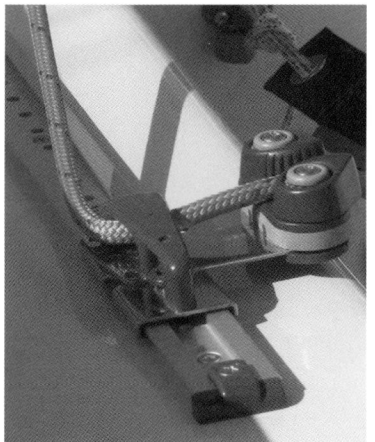

Genoa fairlead, camcleat and track

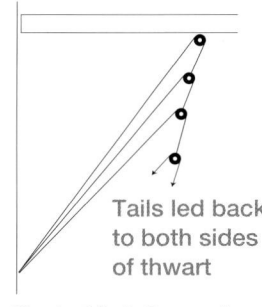

Tails led back to both sides of thwart

Basic 16:1 Cascade Kicker arrangement

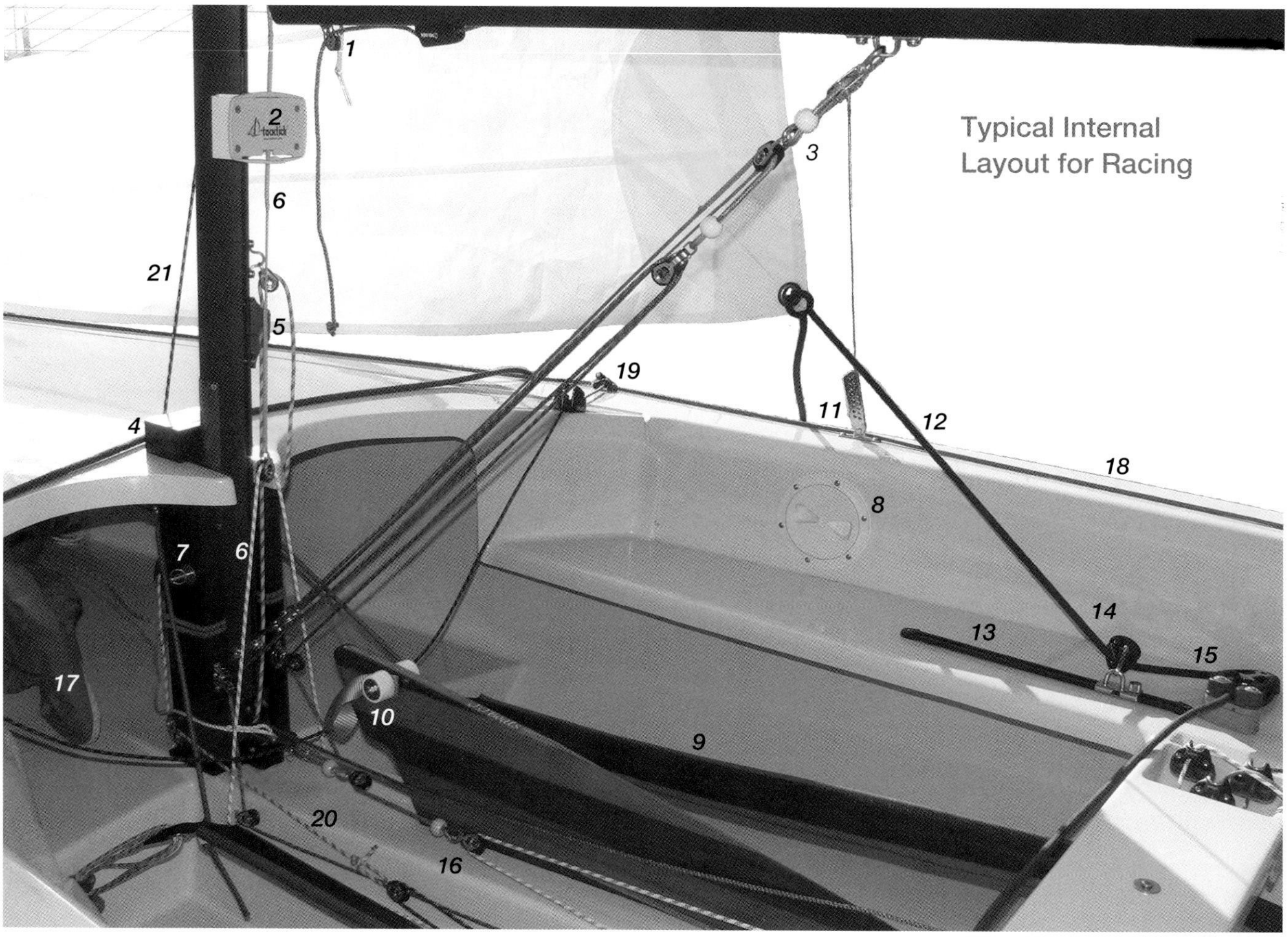

Typical Internal Layout for Racing

1. Mainsail clew outhaul & cleat
2. Digital compass mount
3. Kicking strap cascade type to dual camcleats on thwart
4. Mast chocks
5. Main halyard cleat
6. Cunningham control to dual controls on thwart
7. Mast pin
8. Inspection hatch
9. Toestraps
10. Centreboard stop & strap
11. Shroud adjuster
12. Genoa sheet
13. Genoa track
14. Genoa fairlead
15. Genoa ratchet block & cleat
16. Genoa halyard tensioner (cascade type)
17. Spinnaker
18. Spinnaker sheet
19. Barber hauler (adjustable spinnaker sheet fairlead)
20. Spinnaker pole uphaul
21. Spinnaker pole downhaul

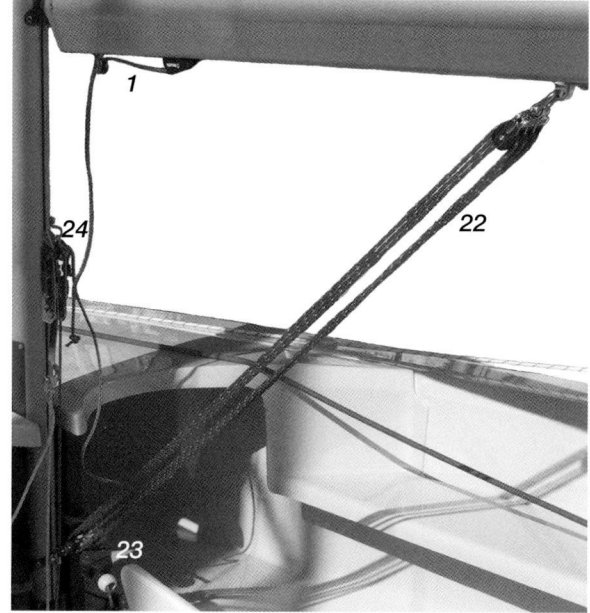

Basic Internal Layout for Day Sailing
(Important - see Page 75 for reefing systems)

22. Kicking strap - pair of triple blocks giving 6:1 purchase
23. Camcleat for kicking strap
24. Genoa halyard tensioner (Highfield lever type)

INTRODUCTION TO WAYFARERS

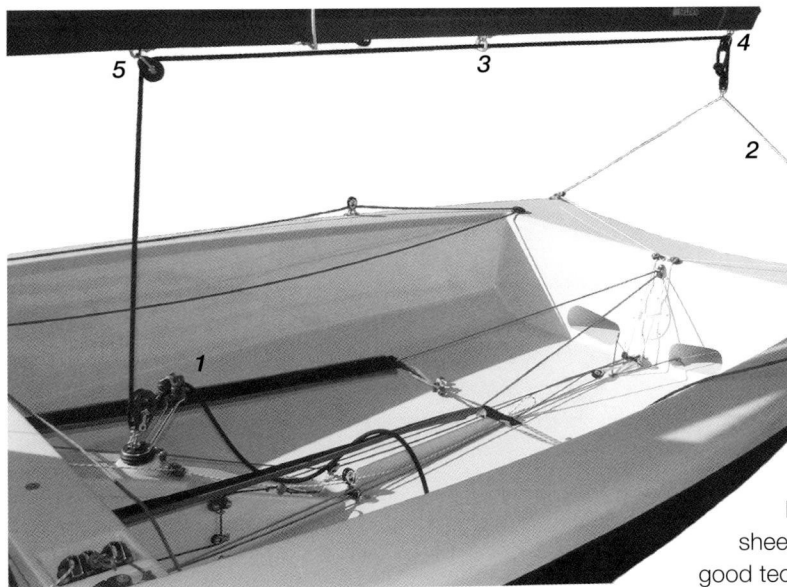

1. Mainsheet ratchet block / swivel jammer
2. Bridle (adjustable at thwart - can be fixed)
3. Retaining loop(s) to hold mainsheet up
4. Block with swivel
5. Blocks attached via boom track fittings

this system makes swapping hands when tacking and gybing easier to master for beginners, as well as providing more space in the cockpit area for family sailing. Both methods may be taught in sailing schools but mastering the centre sheeting method first is probably the best way to develop good technique for future sailing.

Centre Mainsheet System and Bridle

The standard method of running the mainsheet normally used by racers, as well as more serious cruisers, is to lead the mainsheet along the boom and down in front of the helm to a ratchet block and swivel arm jamming cleat. The centre sheeting arrangement has the advantage that the helm faces forward when tacking and gybing, (enabling a constant watch to be kept ahead), and making it possible quickly and easily to adjust, as well as cleat and uncleat, the mainsheet. The centre mainsheet system normally uses a bridle secured via each corner of the transom, this bridle having a mainsheet block at its centre. The bridle replaces the mainsheet track, which was once a standard fixture. If a fixed bridle is used, its length should initially be set such that the mainsheet block will just reach the lower part of the transom when the bridle is hung over the back. Some racers make the length of the bridle adjustable. A single pulley block with universal swivel needs to be used for the mainsheet boom end fitting - the swivel part of the block preventing the rope binding at an angle to the pulley when sailing off-wind. A pulley block is attached to the boom directly above the centre mainsheet swivel and jammer. A sailcloth tube or hoops are normally fitted to the boom between the mainsheet boom pulley blocks to prevent the mainsheet dropping down and causing a problem for the helm. It is advisable to have the best possible quality centre mainsheet ratchet pulley block and jamming system, which always grips positively, yet releases quickly and easily.

Transom sheeting arrangement

Alternatively, the mainsheet can be led directly to the helm from the back, often used for used for learning and day sailing. A single pulley block with becket is attached to the boom, and a double pulley block is attached to a track on the transom. The mainsheet is attached to the becket of the single pulley block, passed through the upper of the two blocks on the double pulley block, back up through the single block on the boom, and finally down through the lower of the blocks on the transom, before being led to the helm. It is said

The Clew Outhaul

Tightening the outhaul reduces the fullness in the foot of the mainsail optimising its shape for upwind work while maximising the mainsail's projected area for downwind work; easing gives full power for reaching courses. The most commonly favoured method is a cascade pulley system within the boom, using two mini blocks to give a 4:1 purchase, with the boom end of the outhaul secured by a hook or shackle through the cringle at the clew of the sail. Alternatively, a single mini-block can be fitted within the boom (giving a 2:1 purchase) with the second purchase of 2:1 being provided by leading the outhaul rope from the outboard end of the boom through the cringle of the clew of the sail (or through a pulley attached to the clew), and back to the end of the boom where its knotted end can be secured in the small slot/hook provided. Overall this gives a 4:1 purchase. For more precise adjustment for racing, these purchases can be doubled to 8:1 by providing split control lines to the thwart for the helm to use on either side of the boat.

The Cunningham

The cunningham helps to bring the flow of the mainsail forward in increasing breezes while at the same time removing creases that can appear in the mainsail close to the mast. The cunningham is rigged with a single line terminated at the gooseneck and passed over a small pulley block or eye attached to the mainsail luff about 225mm above the tack. This gives a purchase of 2:1, which, with another split control line leading to the helm, brings the final purchase to 4:1.

Toestraps

The toestraps should be just long enough to enable the sailors to sit out comfortably. There should also be shock cord tensioning to keep them taut, so that the sailor can find them easily after a tack or gybe. There must also be enough room left between the helm's toestraps to enable him to step between them as he tacks.

Compass

A requirement for cruising or racing. The exact position for the compass is largely a matter of preference, but it is generally easier to steer a compass course if the compass is in continuous vision whilst looking forward - i.e. fitted beneath the boom, or on the foredeck. If it is fitted on the foredeck, it needs to be of a type and shape that will not foul the jib sheets when tacking. The latest compasses are of an electronic digital type, which give a very clear reading of the compass heading. These compasses have convenient mounting brackets for fitting to the mast below the boom, while still allowing outhauls, cunninghams and other ropes to be passed through easily. Of course they still work on the same magnetic field principle as the ordinary compass, and are most accurate when the boat is kept reasonably upright – which it should be anyway! It is important that all iron and steel items like an anchor and chain are stored as far away from a compass as possible.

Sail Limit Bands

Under the Class Rules sail limit bands need to be applied to the mast and boom. They must be available to be seen and checked for class racing and provide a valuable guide to correct sail setting for cruisers too. It will be seen below that Band 1 is needed to ensure the correct mast rake. The sail limit bands (usually tape) not less than 7mm wide need to be fixed at the following positions on the mast: (i) Band 1 with its upper edge 707mm +/- 3mm above the centre of the pivot hole in the mast; (ii) Band 2 with its lower edge 4949mm +/- 7mm above the centre of the pivot hole in the mast; and (iii) Band 3 with its lower edge not more than 5868mm above the upper edge of band 1. A Band 4 should be marked on the boom with its inner edge not more than 3023mm from the aft edge of the mast when in position on the gooseneck.

Setting up the mast correctly

The aim is that when the rig is under tension, the mast is braced securely to the hull at its foot, and held firmly within the three sides of the mast cut-out section of the foredeck (with chocks or mast ram), enabling all the power generated by the sails to be directly transmitted to the hull. This rig tension is achieved by tensioning the jib halyard against the shrouds via a highfield lever or muscle box (traditionally) or more often these days by a cascade system. For racing, the latter two are far more powerful and adjustable than the highfield lever. A rig tension gauge and a tape measure of at least 8m are needed during the following three components of mast set-up. These are interrelated and so need to be repeated until the base settings are achieved:

1. Set the spreader length and angle – this controls the pre-bend in the mast to match the luff curve in the mainsail.

2. Fix the mast foot position and rake – which largely determines the degree of weather helm when sailing.

3. Set the rig tension – which influences the shape of the luff of the genoa and, in conjunction with the spreaders and chocks, determines the amount of pre-bend in the mast.

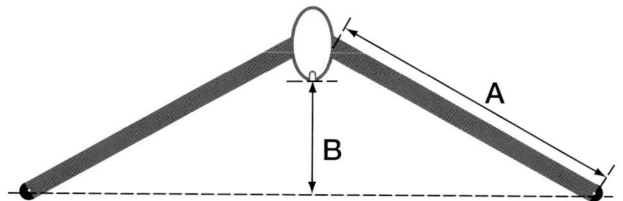

Spreader length and angle
Set A = 508mm and B = 200mm

1. Spreader length and angle

It is essential to set the spreaders up correctly before fitting the mast to the boat. They should be slotted into the mast fittings so that the profile looks like an aircraft wing, (as with the profile of the rudder and the centreboard the finer more pointed edge should be aft!). Each spreader should be set at a length of 508mm measured from the wall of the mast to the shroud. It is very important that the angle of the spreaders is equal on both sides and that the spreaders are securely fixed in position so they are completely rigid – which is not always easy to achieve with the adjustable spreader fittings. To start with, the spreader span (the measurement from shroud to shroud) should be 965mm and the deflection, the distance between the luff groove on the mast and a line running across the spreader span, should be 200mm.

2. Mast foot position and rake

Ensure the mast chocks are removed or that a mast ram if fitted is in its withdrawn position. Then step the mast into the boat, having first ensured that the mast foot track is securely fixed to the base of the tabernacle. With the mast stepped in the boat, a check should be made that all its weight is taken by the mast foot track – rather than the mast pivot pin, thereby allowing the pin to be easily withdrawn. It may be necessary to insert shims under the foot track for this to be achieved. At deck level, it is likely spacers will need to be fitted on either side of the mast slot in the foredeck, to ensure a tight fit for the mast and prevent any sideways movement while still allowing the mast to move forwards or backwards. Now remove the mast pivot pin and pull the mast backwards so the heel of the mast is hard up against the aft pin of the foot track. The genoa can now be hoisted and tensioned, to check the rake of the mast. The muscle box or cascade system linked to the genoa halyard needs to be tightened to achieve a tension in the shrouds of around 150kg – being the amount required for average conditions. With a highfield lever this might be difficult to achieve, in which case use the highest setting possible.

Attach the end of the tape measure to the main halyard and raise it towards the top of the mast to achieve a distance of 5.866m (19ft 3in) from the top of the mast to the middle of band 1 by the gooseneck. With the main halyard cleated at this point, the tape is taken to the stern of the boat to measure the distance from the top of the mast to the top of the transom. On the Mark IV the distance should be in the range 7.240m to 7.290m (23ft 9in to 23ft 11in). For earlier marks the distance should be in the range 7.140m to 7.185m (23ft 5in to 23ft 7in) measured to the bottom of the traveller rail.

1. *Mast pin*
2. *Mast heel and sheaves*
   - *left sheave for jib/genoa halyard*
   - *middle sheave for mainsail halyard*
   - *right sheave for spinnaker halyard*
3. *Mast foot track*
4. *Limit pin*
5. *Genoa wire halyard tail - with hook to cascade tensioner in this example*
6. *Kicking strap anchor point*
7. *Fairleads to take kicker control to thwart (optional)*
8. *Spinnaker pole uphaul fairlead*

The position of the shrouds within the shroud plates may need to be adjusted to achieve this measurement. It is worth checking at this point that the mast is stepped centrally in the boat by using the tape measure to check that the distances from the top of the mast to the port and starboard corners of the transom are equal.

It should now be possible to insert the mast pivot pin without any resistance being felt. The smallest diameter mast pivot pin permitted under Class Rules (6mm – ¼ in) is recommended, in order to allow for maximum movement of the mast without the pin binding in the mast pivot hole at any time. If the pivot pin jams on the front part of the hole through the mast, the limit pin in the mast foot track must be moved forward. If it jams on the back of the hole, then the limit pin needs to be moved back, (or insert packing pieces between the mast foot and the pin – one cent Euro coins being an ideal fit)! The mast pin, which must always be in its place to comply with the class rules, must be completely free within the mast pivot hole, since stresses caused by the mast bearing against the pin can cause stress cracks in the mast and/or tabernacle around the pivot hole.

The final check is for mast pre-bend, which, with the rig under normal tension - 150 kg - is the slight forward curve of the mast relative to a vertical line between the top of the mast and the gooseneck. The main halyard can be used for the vertical line and when pulled taut, should result in a gap between the halyard and the luff groove of the mast at the spreaders of 25 to 38mm (1 to 1.5in). Further guidance on this figure is available from your sail-maker. If further fine adjustment is needed, this can be achieved by adjusting the spreaders. Moving them backwards will increase the mast bend, and moving them forwards will decrease it. The mast pivot pin must always be checked to ensure that it is free to move as the very final part of setting up the mast. If it is not, then the setting up procedure (from adjusting the mast track pin) must be repeated until it is. However, it is always necessary to check after hoisting the sails and tensioning the genoa that the heel of the mast is hard against the mast track pin. If not, reaching up and pushing the mast forward will usually achieve this. Now finally with the rig tension of 150 kg still on, the mast foot back up against

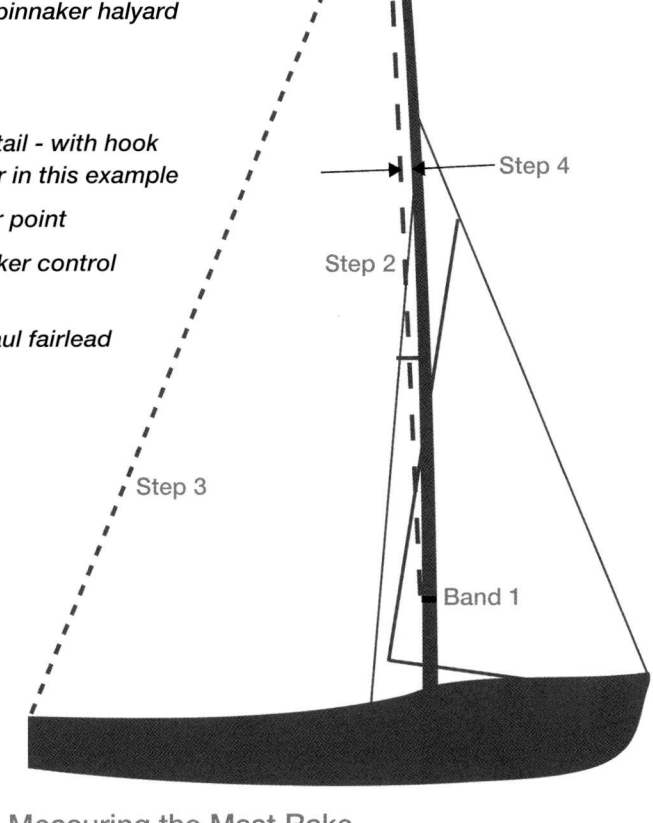

Measuring the Mast Rake

Step 1: Put the genoa up, rig tension on and take a tape measure to the top of the mast with the main halyard.

Step 2: Adjust the halyard so the tape measures 5866mm to the centre of the Band No. 1. (This band should be 707mm above the pivot hole.) Cleat the halyard at this position.

Step 3: Take the tape to the top of the transom and measure the distance. This should be in the range 7240mm to 7290mm for Mark IV and 7140mm to 7185mm for other Marks

Step 4: The halyard can also be used to gauge the pre-bend. For most sails this should be in the 25-38mm range. See also Table 4 - Mast Setup Guide Page 88

the aft pin of the foot track and the mast nicely supported from side to side, it just remains to fit chocks or set the mast ram in front of the mast so that the mast is firmly trapped between the foot pin and the deck.

With the centreboard and mast in the right position and firmly located, the Wayfarer should now be well balanced for fast all-round racing and cruising. If any difficulty is experienced in setting up the mast, then it can be helpful to seek the advice of another experienced local Wayfarer sailor. A useful alternative is to attend a Race Training weekend, or any Wayfarer tuning sessions, where this subject will always be covered.

Table 1. Genoa Setting Guide

Centre of track to centreline		530mm
Genoa fairlead measured to transom	Light winds:	2400mm
	Medium winds:	2380mm
	Heavy winds:	2350mm

Table 2. Mainsail Setting Guide

Mast Rake	Tape measure hauled up on main halyard from top of black band to underside of mainsheet track	7135mm - 7190mm (23' 5" - 23' 7")
Mast Rake (Mk IV)	Tape measure hauled up on main halyard from top of black band to top of transom	7240mm to 7290m (23ft 9in to 23ft 11in)
Spreader Length	Measured from mast-wall to shroud	508mm (1' 8")
Spreader Span	Measured from shroud to shroud	965mm (3' 2")
Spreader Deflection	From luff groove to straight-edge across shrouds	203mm (8")
Pre-Bend	From luff groove to main halyard stretched taut from masthead to mast/gooseneck intersection with rig tension on	25mm - 38mm (1" - 1.5")
Shroud Tension	Light winds	140kg (300lbs)
	Medium winds	150kg (330lbs)
	Heavy winds	160kg (350lbs)

Table 3. Tension/Chock Guide

	Light winds: crew sitting in		Medium winds - crew sitting out		Breezy: spilling wind	
	Flat water	Chop	Flat water	Chop	Flat water	Chop
Rig tension	medium	medium slack	medium tight	medium	very very tight	very tight
Jib sheet tension	fairlead forward sheet eased	fairlead well forward sheet medium eased	fairlead middle sheet medium	fairlead middle	fairlead aft sheet medium	fairlead middle sheet medium
Main sheet tension/ boom end position	boom eased leech eased	boom eased leech eased	boom inboard leech medium	boom slightly eased leech medium tight	boom out, leech very tight	boom out leech tight
Cunningham	nil	nil	nil to moderate	nil to minute	medium	medium
Kicker/vang	very light tension	light tension	moderate tension	medium tension	tight to very tight	very tight
Main foot tension	very tight	slightly eased	slightly eased	well eased	tight	tight
Mast bend	no chocks pre-bend	slightly chocked pre-bend	very chocked mast straight	very chocked mast straight	chocked mast bent	medium chocked mast bent

Rigging the Spinnaker

The Wayfarer has two types of spinnaker: the standard one-design symmetrical spinnaker, as shown right, which, whilst being the most challenging of the sails to handle, is also the most satisfying way to attain maximum performance off-wind – it also happens to be essential for official class racing. The other choice is the asymmetrical spinnaker, which is an option on the Wayfarer World and Mk IV versions of the boat for training and day sailing – it is not used in official class racing. Whilst a spinnaker certainly improves a boat's performance off the wind, it is advisable for newcomers to seek advice from more experienced helms before handling this sail for the first time, and to practise using the sail in lighter wind conditions before trying it out in stronger winds. Training courses are ideal. Hard-won experience in racing is another option!

The Symmetric Spinnaker - Introduction

The standard spinnaker has evolved to work well for beam and broad reaching as well as running. The sails are usually made from 0.75 oz nylon and cut to one of three panel layout designs. The simplest 'cross-cut' or 'orbital' designs have panels running horizontally across the sail. These suffer from slight distortion under pressure from the wind, especially close to the head and the clew patches, making for a less than perfect overall shape when running. The 'tri-radial' has panels coming out of each corner and meeting in the middle. This produces a very stable shape, but is a little deeper in cross-section and hence a good shape when running but is slightly less efficient on a tighter reach. The most popular design for racing is now a radial clew design. This gives good load stability down the line of the cloth for running, with a flatter crosscut shape for reaching. The spinnaker, usually hoisted by the helm, is set to the mast by a halyard through a ball-bearing sheave fitted just above the hounds. Sheets are attached through cringles to the clew corners of the sail. The windward clew of the sail, which becomes the tack, (depending on the tack/gybe being sailed), is set as close as possible to the hook on the end of the spinnaker pole. The other end of the spinnaker pole is hooked on to a 'D' ring on the mast, and the sheet is cleated to maintain the desired angle for the pole. The effect of cleating the windward sheet attached to the spinnaker pole is to stabilise the luff of the spinnaker with respect to the wind strength and angle being sailed.

The Spinnaker Pole System

The maximum length permitted for the pole is 1982mm. The 'D' ring on the front of the mast can be from 350 to 550mm above the gooseneck. The spinnaker pole uphaul controls the height of the pole and needs to be adjustable. Conventionally, the pole is stowed on the boom, in which case the loop system for the uphaul is the normal method. A ramp is fitted at the centre of the pole. When the pole is launched, it is simply slid out. The loop slips up and over the ramp and catches in

the centre groove of the ramp. It can be left there during the gybe and the pole only has to be twisted through 90° when it is being retrieved. It is important that, when stowed, the spinnaker pole does not fall off the boom. The normal method is to push its aft end into a plastic-coated stainless steel loop - one each side - which should be positioned about 1800mm from the gooseneck. It is also a good idea to fit plastic clips at the forward end of the boom to hold the uphaul/downhaul and prevent the pole from shooting forward. A stainless steel eye should be screwed to the top of the pole 100mm from each end of the pole at right angles to the pistons. The piston release cord should be led through these with a couple of knots or ball stoppers beyond. The loop or key ring is thus trapped, and therefore cannot twist off the end of the pole, while the knots/stoppers help the crew to get a grip on the release cord. This is such a standard method that fully-fitted poles are available 'off the shelf'.

The advantages of stowing the pole along the boom far outweigh its small drawback of extra weight on the boom. If the pole is not permanently attached to the boat, it is in fact quite easy to lose it altogether, say, after capsizing. And poles are rather expensive. For those who are day sailing, cruising or on rallies, the system doesn't interfere with the conventional slab reefing system either. (Roller reefing might be a different matter!)

The Spinnaker Pole Fittings

1	Piston hooks	9	Elastic section of downhaul with stopper to prevent pole skying
2	Piston release cord	10	Uphaul led to cleat by rear of centreboard case via 2:1 purchase
3	Knot/ball stopper - helps to grip release cord	11	Spinnaker guy - barber hauler (12) 'on'
4	Guide eye for release cord 100mm from end	12	Barber hauler
5	Ramp to locate uphaul/downhaul	13	Cleat for spinnaker guy on coaming each side
6	Rope uphaul	14	Spinnaker sheet - with barber hauler 'off'
7	Rope downhaul	15	Gooseneck
8	Sheaves at front of mast	16	'D' Ring on mast 350-550mm above gooseneck

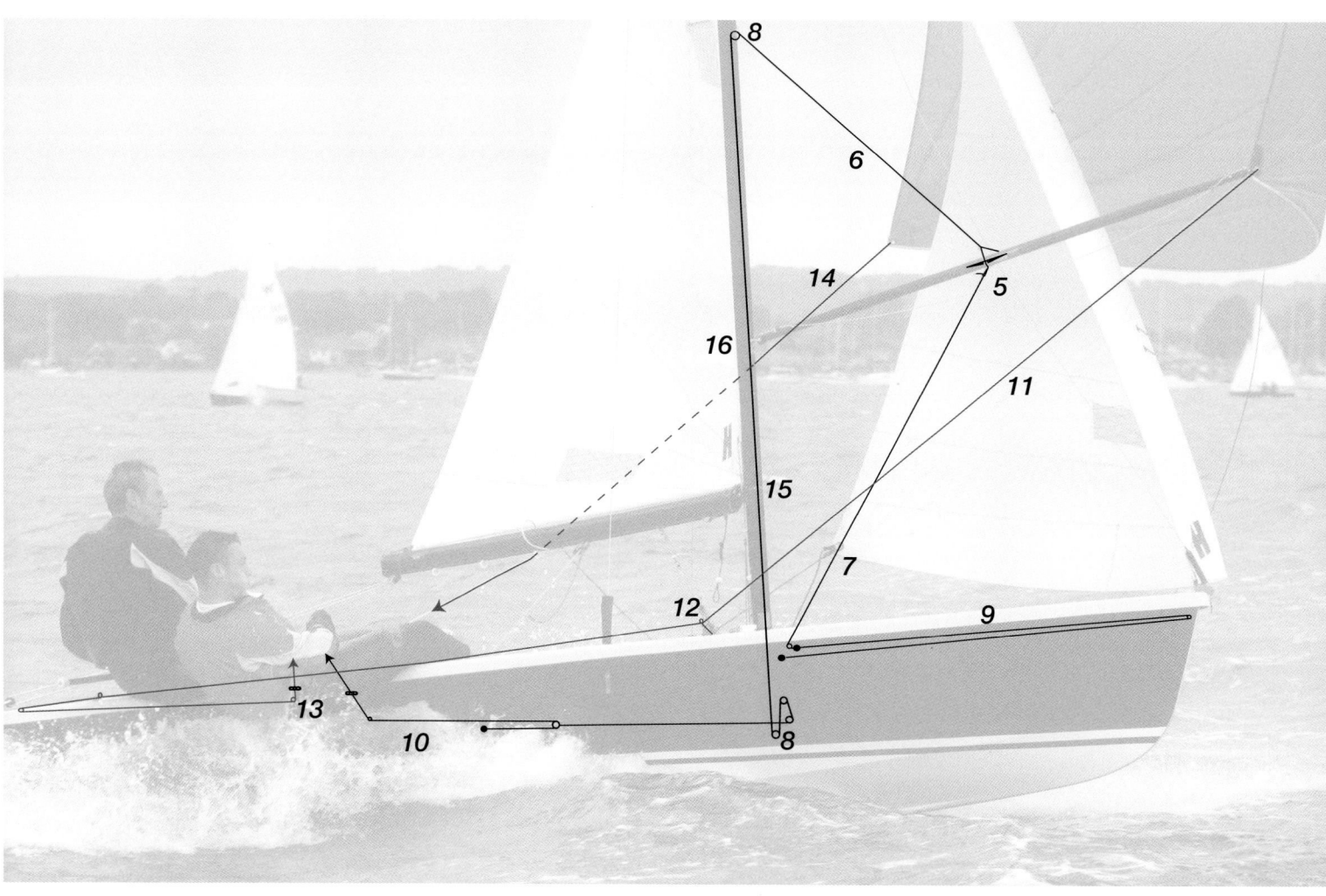

Schematic showing the spinnaker pole uphaul and downhaul system

INTRODUCTION TO WAYFARERS

The pole should always be clipped on to the 'D' ring on the mast with the piston part uppermost. This means that the crew doesn't have to lift the pole up and over when setting the spinnaker, or up and out when lowering. It also means that the spinnaker sheet is running over the solid part at the outer end, and not the piston.

Adjusting the pole height

The pole height is controlled by the pole uphaul. This passes through a sheave on the mast at spreader level. This line emerges from a second sheave at the front of the mast near the heel block, and via turning blocks on the underside of the foredeck and tabernacle to a cleat on the centreboard casing, where it can be controlled by the helm. It is very important that there should be no play in the system when the pole is in position, for there is nothing worse than a pole waving about, making a mockery of leech tension. A downhaul therefore needs to be incorporated. The line for the downhaul is attached to a point near the stern bulkhead (boats with closed front tanks like Mk 1) or more neatly under the foredeck (open fronted boats like World or Mk IV) via a suitable length of shock-cord. The knot where the two are joined is adjusted to a position where it forms a 'limit' stop (often reinforced with a bead or plastic stopper). This stops the spinnaker pole skying. The rope then passes from this point to a turning block alongside the tabernacle and up through an eye in the deck in front of the mast recess (max distance 64mm) and then to the underside of the pole. The elastic must be in the downhaul part so that the spinnaker does not have to support the weight of the pole. It is only necessary to adjust the uphaul part as the shock-corded downhaul takes up any slack when the uphaul is eased off and the pole lowered. Then the downward pull of the sheets keeps the pole from skying. When reaching, you can re-tension the uphaul, stretching the elastic to its knot, and raising the pole to its reaching position. A bit of slack is needed when putting the pole on the mast depending on the strength of the crew – the uphaul can be eased and re-tensioned by the helmsman to allow this.

The Spinnaker Halyard

The spinnaker halyard should be led back to the helmsman on the starboard side from the starboard sheave at the bottom of the mast to a block and cleated near the back of the centreboard case. Care should be taken to get the correct positioning, as the helmsman will have to hoist whilst steering with the tiller between his legs. With the mainsheet cleated, and yards of halyard to pull, he will have more than enough to deal with. The spinnaker needs to be hoisted as high as possible – there is no need, as has been convention, to tie a knot in the halyard just above the head to keep the head away from the mast. Boats with spinnaker chutes will have a continuous halyard which leads back forwards again through the chute and up to the middle of the spinnaker as a downhaul.

Spinnaker sheet arrangements

Spinnaker sheets should be of 6mm low stretch line, which can be tapered at each end to 4mm for lightness – especially beneficial in light air - and ease of attachment to the sail clews. A length of some 15 to 16m is required depending on the mark of boat and the routing of the sheets. The sheet (or leeward spinnaker line) flies from a block or sheave on the aft side deck, with the rear end being led forward under or in front of the side deck coaming and then to the crew via one or more pulley blocks by the thwart. It is essential to keep friction down to a minimum in the control lines set-up. The guy (or windward spinnaker line) can be controlled at deck level near the shroud plates by a reaching hook such as a non-captive type of Clamcleat, which allows the crew to play the guy past the hook and cleat as necessary.

Barber haulers (twinning lines)

An alternative to the reaching hook for the guy is the twinning lines system, otherwise known as the barber hauler. With this system, the sheet runs through a block or ring which is attached to a line running down through a deck eye near the shroud, past cleats each side of the cockpit and out the other side in the same way. Pulling and cleating the windward end of the twinning line pulls the windward spinnaker sheet - the guy - into deck level by the shroud, where the crew can control it. The particular advantage of this system is that it can be pulled on quickly by either helm or crew. Also, in very strong winds, both sides can be partially tensioned to damp down the spinnaker. It also stops the leeward sheet from looping itself over the end of the boom when the sheet is flapping or in gybing manoeuvres. A means of cleating the guy is still needed with this system. Although a cam cleat can be mounted near the shroud it has to be positioned so that it doesn't inadvertently jam when the barber hauler is pulled in. It is more conventional now to put the cam cleat on the vertical face of the coaming above the thwart with the further advantage that the helm can assist – the load on the guy can be considerable! Releasing the leeward side of the barber hauler allows the spinnaker sheet to fly and be controlled from its stern deck sheave.

Spinnaker launching and retrieval methods

There are two ways of stowing and launching the 'kite'.
In older marks the spinnaker is stowed on either side in sailcloth bags in front of the side seats. The sail is usually taken down on whichever is the windward side and stowed on that side. When racing it is helpful to work out what the next spinnaker point of sailing is going to be so that the spinnaker is always lowered on the right side for the next hoist. It is best to arrange that if the next hoist is going to be on a run, the hoist is to windward and if the course is going to be a reach to hoist to leeward. There is more detail later in the book.

Spinnaker Chute

The spinnaker chute facility of the Wayfarer World and the Mark IV has the spinnaker stowed under the foredeck on the port side with the head showing in the chute's opening behind the forestay. Unlike hoisting from spinnaker bags there is no decision making as to which side to hoist or recover the spinnaker from. The spinnaker halyard is used for both hoisting and retrieval by making it into an endless line, which is led through the chute and attached to a reinforced patch at the centre of the sail. When hoisting the spinnaker there needs to be sufficient line to extend to the patch on the front of the spinnaker without restriction. It is necessary on retrieval to ensure the guy and sheet are well controlled as the helm pulls down on the halyard - the pole coming in once the spinnaker is well into the chute.

The spinnaker chute - a feature on the Mark IV.

Twin Spinnaker Pole Systems

Wayfarers normally use a single spinnaker pole arrangement as described on Page 16. But twin pole systems with a pole stowed each side of the boom are sometimes seen. The system has the advantage that there is always a pole on the windward side for the crew to reach. Before a gybe the windward pole is released and self-stows to the boom using an elasticated arrangement. After the gybe the new windward pole is used. This differs from the conventional method of swapping pole ends during a gybe. More complex systems have a launching system for the poles too.

Dropping the spinnaker to windward - the normal procedure with spinnaker bag launching.

An optional 'spinnaker sock' keeps the spinnaker tidy and away from under the crew's feet. Note also the handy pocket. At the opening is a plastic bead forming a ring to keep the 'mouth' open so that the the kite can enter without restriction. The sock is open at the back - this enables the downhaul to pass through to its normal block under the bottom of the thwart.

An asymmetric spinnaker on a Wayfarer Mk IV

The Asymmetric Spinnaker

As its name suggests, the asymmetric spinnaker has permanent luff and leeches of unequal length - like a huge lightweight genoa, but sheeted in to the rear quarters. Its halyard is set from the same mast sheave as the halyard of a symmetrical spinnaker. It is gybed downwind on a pole or bowsprit coming out of the bow using its sheets – somewhat similar to gybing with a genoa. The development of this sail originates from skiff sailing, where speeds were attained that caused the apparent wind to move so far forward that a conventional spinnaker would collapse. Indeed, speeds exceeding true wind velocity were sometimes possible while allowing quick course changes from gybe to gybe.

The Wayfarer obviously doesn't have the design performance of a skiff, and the advantage of an asymmetric is limited to being much easier to set than a normal spinnaker and slightly enhancing the off-wind speed. However, it doesn't perform as well as a symmetrical spinnaker when running directly downwind. Nevertheless, the asymmetric is a simple-to-set and fun option popular with sailing schools and family day sailors. The set-up for the latest asymmetric rig enables the pole to shoot out whilst hoisting the spinnaker, meaning that complete launching is achieved in one operation. As with the chute system for the normal spinnaker, the halyard is extended and attached to a reinforced patch at the centre of the asymmetric as one continuous line. The pole may be

Detail showing the launch system for the asymmetric spinnaker pole on a Mark IV. The guides which enable the pole to be swung to windward can be seen.

angled to windward, which allows the helm to sail further off wind. Trimming the sail is the same as with a normal spinnaker. However, in order to achieve the maximum downwind speed, sailing the correct course to the wind, depending on its angle and strength, becomes much more critical for the helm.

SAILING FAST & EFFECTIVELY

In recent years, the Wayfarer has developed into an exciting and demanding racing dinghy even more so now with the introduction of the new Mark IV. Exciting, not in the sense of an out-and-out planing trapeze dinghy, but rather in the sense that it responds so beautifully to correct, accurate control - facilitated by such a lovely light helm which precisely and instantly conveys the boat's 'feelings'. In this section, the characteristics of the Wayfarer as a racing boat are looked into, with an introduction to the points of sailing followed by a fairly detailed look at using the various sail controls to get boat speed. Developing good technique is beneficial to cruisers too, helping to instill confidence in all conditions. The ability to sail reasonably fast to windward to get around a headland before the tide turns or to be able to manoeuvre smoothly and efficiently are vitally important for safety and good use of the wind and tides available. Keeping well up with a rally group is also a great help to the rally organisers too! Some of the topics will to a certain extent overlap and this should help to reinforce some of the ideas presented. There is quite a lot to take on board and it therefore useful to use the information as a reference to dip into after every race. Once perfected, new champions should be in the making! The UKWA and its international sister class associations hold training courses from time to time in which coaches give the fullest possible attention to the specific details of setting up the boat, sail controls and boat trim as well as general tactics, rules and race strategy. It is recommended that crews attend an 'Introduction to Racing' course at their home club beforehand, in order to benefit fully from class training courses. However, nothing beats time on the water in club racing and at open meetings. A characteristic of the class is its friendly nature: after stiff competition on the water, details of boat settings and tactics can be discussed over a drink at the bar – there is always something to learn, no matter how experienced or inexperienced one is!

Type of Boat

All types of Wayfarer are suitable for racing – though it has to be said that some are a little more suitable than others! It is recognised that a new boat is likely to have a slight performance advantage over an older boat – it will be down to the minimum weight with a nice smooth hull. Another recognised performance advantage is for the hull to be as stiff as possible – otherwise some of the energy from the rig is lost by the hull panels flexing or 'panting', especially in waves. When looking for the ideal version of Wayfarer to race therefore, a new Mk IV foam sandwich 'racing' version would be the most obvious choice. If that choice is limited to the second-hand market, then a sound wooden Wayfarer, preferably with a good racing track record, or alternatively a 'Plus S' model which incorporates foam stiffening, would be ideal. The most important factor in getting optimum boat speed, however, is not the type of Wayfarer being sailed, but the ability of the helm and crew sailing it. Provided the boat has been set up well, a top racing crew could sail any type of Wayfarer fast enough to be somewhere up with the front of the fleet; conversely, the latest 'top of the range' racing Wayfarer, with every item of 'go faster' gear allowed, will not propel a less experienced crew from the back or mid-fleet to the front. It is most important to ensure a Wayfarer hull used for racing is towards the minimum weight allowed within the class rules. All Wayfarers have the potential to derive the same power from the rig, and if your boat is heavier than the next, it will obviously not accelerate as quickly or sail as fast. (Having said that, the Wayfarer is extremely tolerant of different crew weights - as long as this is positioned appropriately!) When purchasing a second hand boat for racing, avoid a plastic one where the hull has been painted, or those with a wooden or rubber gunwale fend-off, as these add unnecessary weight. As the first stage of preparing a boat for racing, it is worth turning the hull over, preferably mounting it on trestles, and carrying out a thorough inspection for damage, particularly along the keel and bilge keels. It is also sensible to take all the fittings off to make sure that they are properly anchored – you will be driving the boat harder than it has ever been sailed before!

Wayfarer Mk IV

There has tended to be a general belief that wooden Wayfarers have a competitive edge on GRP versions, though this was far more likely due to the self-perpetuating folklore of top helms choosing wooden boats than the type of boat itself. The latest Mk IV racing version with its stiffened hull is designed to be 'as fast as the fastest' - there is no longer any reason to believe that the wooden boat has any performance advantage. As we go to press, early results since the launch of the Mk IV show that class racing between the main racing types is closer than ever. Wayfarers have always been regarded as very stable and seaworthy boats, but racers have reported that the Mk IV has particularly excellent stability and assured handling characteristics, giving them extra confidence for fast off-wind sailing in windy conditions. The more comfortable side decks make it easier for the crew to hike out further, and for longer periods, making beating upwind slightly less demanding for some crews. The boat is by far the easiest to recover after a capsize, enabling the boat to be sailed 'dry' at all times. In short, the Mk IV has been designed to incorporate all the best features of previous designs plus a few ergonomic advantages, and is therefore the most ideal version to purchase for anyone keen on racing. However, if one is relatively new to sailing it may be better to 'cut one's teeth' on an older, less expensive version first.

Fast sailing techniques

Proper technique is important for successful Wayfarer racing. Luckily, the factors which influence Wayfarer boat speed are now well known – governed as they are by the specific characteristics of the Wayfarer, these factors revolve around:

1. Keeping the relatively heavy hull with its large wetted area moving as quickly as possible in all conditions;

2. The need to keep the air flowing smoothly over the large, low aspect ratio sail plan without the air stalling and without the boat heeling too much;

3. The requirement to ensure that the aft-raked centreboard creates the maximum possible resistance to leeway and that the rather small rudder blade steers the boat, even in the strongest of breezes. With their parallel sides and short bevels, both the foils will stall all too easily if not properly used.

4. And a combination of the above - wherever possible, help the rudder by using the sails. If you want to bear away, ease the mainsheet to bring the centre of effort forward. If you need to luff up into the wind, ease the jib very slightly, this will bring the centre of effort further aft.

The Sails

The sails are the driving force of the boat - clearly good sails are one of the most important considerations for top performance. For optimum boat speed, the air needs to flow over the surface of the sails as smoothly as possible – the smoother the flow, the greater the speed they will generate. For newcomers to Wayfarer racing it is perhaps advisable to make the best use of the original sails for the first season, and seek advice from those on the racing circuit before buying new sails for the next season. Where possible it is useful to retain the older suit of sails for non-racing use, as well as for racing in stronger wind conditions. This will greatly extend the life of the newer set of sails. Never let the sails - particularly the genoa - flog whilst rigging the boat or when idling at sea. This quickly spoils the shape of the sail. It is advisable to wrap the genoa loosely around the forestay immediately it has been hoisted to stop it flogging, and to take the sails down as soon as sailing is finished. If idling at sea, it is best to 'heave-to', with the genoa backed and the tiller hard over to leeward.

Sail Controls

Most of our concerns with rigging and tuning relate to getting the boat to sail fast to windward for which there are obviously three components, speed, pointing ability and leeway. The sail controls below give a guide as to how the optimal combination of these can be achieved. And there will be times when one of these has to be sacrificed, possibly for tactical reasons, for example (i) you may want to point very high and are willing to sacrifice some speed to get into some clear air or (ii) you may want to accelerate fast away from the start-line to get into a good position and not worry too much about pointing. This can be effectively controlled by the mainsail leech. An open leech allows for speed while a tight leech is required for pointing. At any rate speed - first gear - must be obtained before moving into second gear - pointing. In light winds second gear may not be advisable – speed being paramount. To achieve all this, additional fittings may be needed to give greater mast and sail control than would be necessary for basic sailing - though nothing more than described in the first chapter. But in order that these operate smoothly and reliably, the controls need to be of the highest quality.

Setting the Genoa

It is essential to use a genoa with a luff wire for optimum boat performance. The luff wire must be able to be tensioned by either a muscle box or a cascade system in order to obtain a load on the shrouds of between 140 and 160 kg (300-350lbs). The genoa's own luff tension can be adjusted separately on the luff wire by means of a thin length of rope around the tack cringle and plastic cleat on the luff of the sail. It should not be tensioned so that it is tight, or in any way stretched. Ideally, it will be sufficiently loose for small wrinkles to appear from the luff throughout its length. It is inadvisable to use any genoa-furling device for racing, since the bottom of the genoa should be as close as possible to the foredeck, in order to prevent the air flow escaping between the foot and the foredeck. The front of the genoa is responsible for aligning the air flow over the rest of the sail plan. Therefore, getting the angle of attack right is vital, while at the back, the leech has to deflect and

then squeeze the air through the slot between the genoa and the mainsail. If the leech is too tight, the air gets stalled, and if it is too slack, the air is not squeezed enough. Telltales are attached to the luff of a racing genoa so that the helm can ensure there is a smooth flow of air over both windward and leeward surfaces. Some helms find it helpful to distinguish between the windward and leeward telltales by off-setting one side 50mm higher than the other. This can be particularly helpful in bright sunshine conditions, when the telltales will show up better in silhouette. The telltales are normally positioned ¼, ½, and ¾ along the genoa luff, though it is more important to ensure they are spaced an equal distance apart, are approximately 230mm from the luff wire, and are positioned away from any of the genoa seams to prevent them from snagging. The genoa telltales are key; the genoa must be set so that the air can move from its leading edge through to the leech of the main with as little interference as possible. The angle of attack of the genoa must therefore be constant throughout its height, with the three sets of telltales collapsing at the same time. If the top one collapses first, the genoa leech needs to be tightened by moving the pulley block of the genoa fairlead forward. If the bottom one collapses first the pulley block will need moving aft to tighten the foot. Of course tightening or easing the genoa sheet also affects the telltale balance!

When beating to windward, the optimum boat performance will be obtained when the windward telltales are all angled upwards between 30° and 45°. This is because of the action of the boat going through the water, which will tend to push the air upwards whilst it is flowing over the surface of the sail. The helm should always use the bottom telltale as the reference point. It is the crew's responsibility to set the genoa so that all the telltales are working in unison. It is helpful to make a mark on the genoa sheets, by sewing in coloured whipping thread, at the optimum place for correct sheeting point when close hauled, so that this position can be obtained quickly and easily on each tack.

Another important factor is for the airflow to exit the genoa slot with the minimum back-winding of the mainsail. In order to ensure a smooth airflow between the two sails, the middle of the genoa leech should be set parallel with the centreline of the boat, (so that it is aiming at the inside edge of the side deck at the transom). This is particularly relevant in light winds. It is a very common for the crew to oversheet the genoa, which not only closes the slot, causing the genoa leech to 'choke' the main, but also stalls the airflow over the leeward side of the genoa. Easing the genoa sheet by around 25mm (ensuring that it does not cause any collapse of the top of the genoa), and opening the slot, will lead to an immediate increase in speed. Racing genoas are usually fitted with a telltale ¾ of the way up the leech near the spreader height which can be seen through a corresponding window in the mainsail. This can prove an easier method of finding the most optimum setting for the genoa, particularly in light winds. The genoa sheet is pulled in until the leech telltale is on the verge of being sucked behind the genoa, before easing the sheet out a fraction.

After the tack - the genoa is nicely eased for acceleration as the boat is brought upright.

It is important that the leading edge of the genoa is directly pointed into the wind. Pointing too high will angle the wind to the leeward side of the genoa and will cause it to luff, with the windward telltales collapsing. Pointing too low will angle the wind towards the windward side of the genoa, losing considerable lift, (and hence power), and causing the leeward telltales to collapse. In steady wind conditions, the genoa halyard can generally be highly tensioned to give the leading edge of the genoa a flatter entry curve (since, with the luff wire held at only the top and bottom of its length, there will always be some curve to the luff wire in the vertical plane). This will enable the boat to be sailed higher, whilst still maintaining the correct entry angle for the wind. However an overly tensioned genoa halyard can result in the telltales collapsing inconsistently. This is because a small amount of curvature is built into the sail itself. In this situation, most likely caused by a drop in wind, the genoa halyard needs to be eased to increase the entry curve, which allows for a wider variation of pointing, whilst still being at the correct entry angle to the wind. There is obviously a trade-off between a highly tensioned genoa halyard giving good pointing, but inefficient overall lift, and an eased genoa halyard giving slightly poorer pointing, but more efficient use of the genoa to provide power and windward lift.

Setting the Mainsail

Chapter 1 showed the mast set-up which is the basis for adjusting the sail controls described in this chapter. It is well worth starting a log book – the first entry can be confirmation of the spreader width, mast rake and pre-bend achieved together with a note of the mast foot pin position, the position of the pins in the shroud adjusters and the rig tension! From this each racer may progress to a state of boat-tuning which suits themselves, their crew, and their sails, allowing for various wind strengths and sea states. This is where the log book updated after each race and change of settings can be invaluable. But it is useful to be able to go back to base settings when all else fails! The basic rig set-up with the mast's pre-bend tuned to the sail-maker's lovingly developed curve on the front of the mainsail should provide the fullest sail and therefore maximum power that the crew sitting flat-out can manage. The sail should just flow naturally away from the mast as if they were made for each other! One easy way to confirm this is to turn the boat on its side in a sheltered spot and look closely how the mainsail falls away from the mast with its maximum draft somewhere around halfway over the width of the sail. Adjust the mainsail halyard so that it isn't too tight to achieve this – you will see how over-tightening it produces an unwanted crease behind the mast. Ideally, the halyard should be lightly tensioned in order to allow a line of small wrinkles to emanate from the length of the luff rope. At the same time other controls below can be adjusted to see how they can spoil that lovely shape! While this is a useful exercise it is a pretty inconvenient method to use all the time. A quicker way to check we have the right pre-bend is to check the position of the draft of the mainsail:

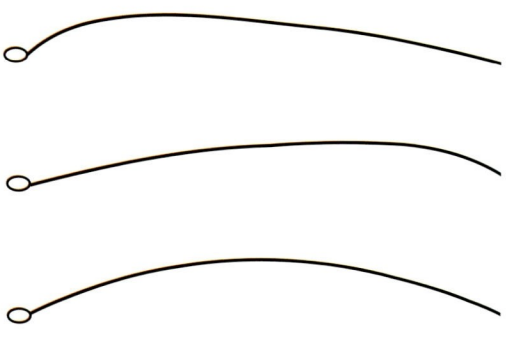

TOP: If the mast has too little bend, the draft in the main will be too far forward.

MIDDLE: If the mast has too much bend, the forward part of the main will be flattened, moving the draft too far aft.

BOTTOM: The right amount of mast bend puts the draft in the central part of the sail as the sail maker intended.

Ideally, we would now just like to take our new found optimal shape out onto the water and keep it that way for maximum speed. In practice though it will be found that in light winds the sail will be too full and the breeze will be reluctant to make its way around the sail's deep curve. Conversely, in heavy winds the sail will be too powerful, and a way of de-powering the rig to maintain maximum speed is necessary. In medium winds the sail should be fine – this will be taken as the starting point for rig control. But first a brief reminder of the sail controls we have available:

The mast ram (or chocks) together with the spreader angle and the amount of rig tension set on the muscle box or cascade system controls the mast pre-bend - and so the maximum draft of the sail.

The kicking strap (vang) adjusts the leech tension and twist in the sail by pulling down on the boom.

The clew outhaul adjusts the fullness (the amount of curve or camber) in the lower part of the sail.

The cunningham tensions the luff of the sail and can be used to flatten the top part of the sail.

The bridle governs how much leech tension we get when we pull in the boom amidships with the mainsheet; but beware the bridle setting isn't being overridden by too tight a kicker.

Of course nothing is so simple and all these controls interrelate – adjusting one may suggest adjustment of another! So let us go back to our medium wind condition:

Medium winds

Medium winds are ones which enable a beat to windward to be maintained with the crew sitting flat out and the boat absolutely flat but without the need to spill wind. The mast needs to maintain its pre-set position with all the chocks in (or mast ram set) as determined in the mast-set-up. The outhaul should also be moderately tight with the cunningham off at this stage. Once beating to windward (with the kicking strap and bridle well eased at this stage) it will be noted that as the mainsail is pulled in towards the centreline the boom will lift and the top of the sail will fall away to leeward generating little power. Something is needed to get the power back into the sail and reproduce our wanted shape. The kicking strap could be used – but unfortunately it not only pulls the boom down – it also pushes the mast forward, over-cooking our carefully set up mast pre-bend and consequently spoiling the shape of the mainsail too. This is where the bridle comes in. The bridle enables the boom to be pulled in towards the centre-line of the boat with the mainsheet, while allowing some control over the tightness of the leech and hence the angle of the top batten. The bridle needs to be pulled in, symmetrically with respect to both sides, until when the mainsheet is in, the mainsheet blocks are touching (block to block) and the top batten is parallel to the centre-line of the boat. This brings the mainsail back into its designed and most powerful shape. For those with a fixed bridle, this will be a bit of a fiddle untying and retying knots. But, once achieved, the position can be fixed. Some racers prefer the simplicity of such a fixed bridle, which enables the helm to judge the relative position of the boom instantly – say on a new tack when beating to windward. The increasingly fashionable alternative is to make the bridle adjustable with the leads brought forward either side of the thwart. The mainsail should now have a nice bit of twist when viewed from behind – the leech parallel to the boom (or centre-line with the boom sheeted in) at the top batten but curving in towards the bottom near the boom.

Light winds

When the wind is so light that the boat can be kept flat with the crew inboard, the top batten may actually point to windward and the tight leech will trap what breeze there is – the sail might look like a huge bag. What is needed is to flatten the sail and open out the leech to make it as easy as possible for the wind to move over its surface. This is achieved by increasing the pre-bend 5 to 10 mm more by removing mast chocks or withdrawing the mast ram a bit. The outhaul should be tight but again the kicker has to be right off to avoid the dreaded leech tension. For those with an adjustable bridle, this can be eased so that mainsheet block to block can continue to be achieved with minimal down-force on the leech – the boom will be higher than in its medium breeze setting. In light conditions speed and hence less leeway will be made by easing the sheets and not trying to point at all.

Strong winds

When the wind is so strong sailing to windward that sheets have to be eased, even with the crew sitting flat out, then the mainsail needs to be depowered. The solution is firstly to increase pre-bend by withdrawing the mast ram, (or removing mast chocks) to a depth of 10 to 15mm. This flattens the sail, opening up the leech. Tension in the kicking strap is then increased to keep the top batten parallel to the boom – this has the side effect of further increasing mast bend as the kicker pushes the mast forwards, flattening the lower sections of the main and helping to reduce back-winding from the genoa. Of course the mainsheet has to be eased to deal with the gusts accordingly, at all times keeping the boat dead flat. As the kicker is taking much of the load, the mainsheet still has very little weight on it and the mainsheet can concentrate on its main job of positioning the boom at the proper angle to the centre line. The bridle, if adjustable, could be tightened to provide a bit more downward pull on the leech via the mainsheet though it is likely that in breezy conditions the boom will be eased out towards the quarters anyway. As mentioned above the mainsail will have been hoisted with just enough tension to ensure there is no slack in its luff rope – ideally it should show short horizontal wrinkles just at the back of the mast. As the wind rises in strength and the kicker has gradually been brought in to flatten the sail, more horizontal creases will appear. This is when the cunningham comes into play. As the wind rises further, the point of maximum fullness in the sail will move aft, leading to more heeling force and less forward

Powering up to windward in a good breeze. The boom is eased out over the quarter and a tight kicker is keeping the mainsail flat and the slot between the genoa and the mainsail open.

impulse. A tighter cunningham will bring this fullness forward to the preferred mid position also compensating for any additional luff wrinkles caused by kicker-induced over-bending of the mast. If mast over-bending is a persistent problem it may be better to angle the mast spreaders further forward (giving a measurement of around 990mm between the spreaders) so that the mast bends less when greater kicker tension is applied. This provides better leech tension, giving better pointing ability. Needless to say, it is absolutely essential to release the cunningham as soon as the boat is no longer overpowered, as forgetting to ease it is likely to have a greater adverse effect on overall boat speed than not putting it on in the first place. The same goes for the kicker too.

Putting it all together

In practice, the conditions are never as ideal as above but changing constantly in any race. Before the race, the rig can be set to the likely conditions. Thereafter the mainsail leech is the most important aspect of windward sailing. The tighter the leech can be set without over-sheeting the main and stalling the air as it exits the leech, the better the distance that can be made to windward. Over-sheeting the main not only causes a backward force (or drag), but also increases the heeling forces, both of which reduce boat speed. Remember, the mainsail needs to be set so that the leech at the top batten is parallel to the centre-line of the boat when the boom is sheeted in. To set the mainsail correctly initially, the mainsheet should be used to set the boom at the necessary angle for the wind direction, with the twist of the main being adjusted by the bridle (if adjustable) and kicker until the top batten telltale is about to stall. Over-tightening the kicker causes too much low-down mast bend - shortening the bridle and reducing the relative kicker tension prevents this. Once up to good speed, the main can be pulled in far enough for the top telltale to start being sucked in behind the main. Increasing amounts of kicker should be used to prevent the boat being overpowered as the wind strength increases, with the main being sheeted in as far as possible, without putting excessive heel on the boat and/or stalling the air as it exits the leech. The better the boat speed that can be attained, the more effective the centreboard becomes, which in turn improves the pointing angle – remember speed first (first gear) then pointing (second gear) – vice versa just stalls the boat! Probably the most difficult situation is in fluky or gusty conditions, when the sail needs constant adjustment to allow for the variations in speed of the air flowing over it. It is best to follow Michael McNamara's advice in such circumstances, 'if in doubt, ease'. In the same vein, as the wind decreases, don't forget to release the kicker and or cunningham correspondingly to maintain sail shape and power. It is important when coming off the wind onto a reach or run to release the kicker and allow the leech to twist open. Failing to do this will result in excessive weather helm as you try to change course, inevitably slowing the boat. There can be situations where the top batten telltale cannot be used. This occurs when they are too wet, or there is too little wind, as well as in strong winds when the kicker is strongly tensioned to prevent being overpowered, as the telltales will no longer stall. In this situation it is best to watch for the basic essential of keeping the upper leech batten parallel to the boom when beating.

Keeping her flat

Keeping the boat upright is perhaps the single most important aspect of Wayfarer boat speed. If the boat is allowed to heel, the water has to travel around asymmetrical curves; the waterline is shortened and the stern digs in. Not only does the boat go slowly, but it is also hard to steer with massive weather helm, and then the boat goes sideways as the centreboard loses its grip. A check needs to be kept for telltale vortices coming off the leeward chine at the transom, which denote the boat is not perfectly upright. A watch for these needs to be kept at all times, but is most likely to occur when

Heeling the boat may sometimes feel fast - but it isn't! Ease the main and then check the rig is set right for the conditions.

running, with the helm sitting to leeward. The motto has to be "keep the burgee above the crew's head". This is obviously achieved by easing out the mainsheet to reduce the amount of curvature in the main as soon as the boat heels. In extreme circumstances, the genoa should go out, too. The proper technique is to watch the gust coming towards the boat, decide whether it is going to head or lift, and then, as it hits, have the sheet ready to ease, i.e. un-cleat the sheet. As soon as the boat heels, ease and keep easing, even if the main is backing. Once the gust has eased, the main can be sheeted in again. The way to decide whether the approaching gust is a header or a lift is straightforward. If the gust front looks closer to the bow than it does to the side, then the gust will be a header. If the front appears to be closer to the side than to the bow, then it will be a lift. In fact, it doesn't matter what happens as the gust hits, as long as the sailors are prepared for its arrival. This system works best if both helm and crew remain fairly still and sitting out. If either of the sailors keeps diving inboard too early, then the boat is unstable, and the sails cannot be sheeted correctly. There is no need to keep moving about anyway, because if the boat heels to windward, then all that is needed is to sheet the main in to lift the sailors up out of the water. The only exception to the upright rule is in very light winds. Here the boat needs to be heeled just enough to get the sails to set rather than flop about.

Fore and aft trim

The fore and aft position of the crew is also very important. The aim of fore and aft balance is for the bottom of the transom to be just out of the water, so that there is the least possible disturbance of water as it exits the stern. There is a tendency for crews to sit too far forward when beating, leaving the transom too high.

Roll Tacking: The secret is for both sailors to remain on the old windward side until the boom has gone over

Roll Tacking

The Wayfarer will roll tack beautifully without stopping. The secret of a good tack is for both sailors to remain on the old windward side until the boom has gone over. Then both sailors should move to the new windward side. It is also important to ease the mainsheet a little as the helm goes across. This gives time for the sailors to sit down after the tack without the boat heeling too much. The crew should be marginally behind the helm so that he can, in windy conditions, sit down on the weather side, or in light conditions, move back to the leeward side as needed. The crew should face aft when tacking in order to pass under the kicking strap more easily, and bring the windward genoa sheet across to the new side to ease in the final amount of genoa sheet, in order to get the boat quickly up to speed on the new tack. Especially in light winds, the helm is usually unbalanced at this time, and must be careful how he sits down. If he is too clumsy, the air will be shaken off the sails. The helm faces forward while tacking. He shouldn't swap hands until he has sat down on the new windward side, even though this means steering with his hand behind his back for a second or two.

Gybing

The Wayfarer is incredibly stable and can be gybed even in the very strongest breezes. The gybing technique obviously varies according to wind strength and whether or not the spinnaker is being used. In light winds the boat will roll gybe using techniques basically similar to those used in roll tacking, in that the helm and crew wait until the boom goes across before moving across the boat. This has the particular advantage of heeling the boat slightly on the new gybe to keep the mainsail quiet. The gentler the sailors' movements in these conditions, the better. The crew should hold the boom out after the gybe to prevent it coming back into the centre. The kicker too, should be well eased, but not so much that the boom jumps off the gooseneck. In windier conditions, the helm should be in control. As the helm bears away, the crew should move to the centre of the boat, and then stay there until the helm is ready for him to move. This means that the helm knows exactly where the crew is, and can then get him to move to whatever side is needed. It pays the helm to sheet in a fraction as he bears away. Then he can ease the sheet as the boom goes out on the new side. This acts as a spring on the mainsail which otherwise fills quite violently. The moment the boom goes across, the helm should urgently tug the tiller so that the bow is pushed in the same direction as the boom for an instant. Then he should almost immediately straighten the helm. This stops the violent spin towards the wind which so often causes the broach and/or capsize. For this reason, it is best not to throw the boat around too quickly when gybing from reach to reach in a breeze. Arrive at the gybe mark slightly high, bear away onto a dead run, gybe, and then harden up after the spinnaker is sorted out.

Left: Completing the roll tack; the helm is now ready to swap hands - after the tack the helm briefly has his original hands on the tiller extension and the mainsheet, so is here seen steering with the extension behind his back.

Spinnaker Handling

Leeward hoist - from spinnaker bag
Always check the course and rig the spinnaker so that it will be to leeward for the first reach. Always plan to hoist to leeward on subsequent reaches too - possibly by putting in an extra gybe on a run before taking the spinnaker down. The leeward hoist is much safer and simpler. Free the halyard and the sheets. Cleat the uphaul for the approximate pole height desired as per markings in the guy. Adjust the main, jib and centreboard for the new course to keep up boat speed before hoisting. In stronger winds, ease the main and raise the centreboard most of the way before hoisting so as to keep the boat under control until helm and crew can sit out. The helm hoists the spinnaker. The crew slides the uphaul/downhaul to the middle of the pole, and then hooks the pole to the mast. While the crew is doing this, the helm hikes the boat flat.

Windward hoist - from spinnaker bag
If the spinnaker is on the windward side it must be hoisted first with the crew putting the pole in afterwards. Bear away to a broad reach then set the main, jib and centreboard. Cleat the guy to the "preset" mark. The crew frees the halyard and sheet, takes the sheet in one hand then gathers the sail up in a ball and throws it to windward of the forestay as the helm quickly hoists. Immediately after throwing out the sail, the crew quickly trims the sheet so as to pull the sail around behind the jib. The helm takes the spinnaker sheet, keeping it trim, heads up to the proper course, and re-adjusts the main. The crew installs the pole then re-adjusts the sheet and guy. It just remains to re-trim the jib, adjust the centreboard and go!

Retrieving into spinnaker bag
Always bring the spinnaker down to windward. The crew hands the sheet to the helm, stands up, and unhooks the pole from the mast. The crew then pulls the pole aft, releases the uphaul/downhaul and slides the pole into the supports along the boom, then releases the guy. The helm releases the sheet, the crew pulls in the guy, gathers in at least half of the foot of the sail and tells the helm to release the halyard. The crew finally drops the sail into the storage bag.

Spinnaker chute hoisting
Because of the spinnaker chute there is no real difference between a windward or leeward spinnaker hoist. The key to successful spinnaker hoisting is to make sure that everything is properly set up before you start – before even getting on the water. All lines need to run round the outside. In particular watch out for the starboard sheet (which needs to go all the way round the front of the forestay) and make sure that both the halyard and the downhaul lead straight down to the port side of the forestay. Before hoisting, make sure that both sheet and guy are cleated amidships (with twinning line arrangements) or are held in the reaching cleats. Only when ready to hoist does the crew ensures that the sheet is running free. The crew clips the pole end onto the guy and locks the uphaul/downhaul into position (not yet clipping to mast). The helm moves into the centre of the boat, steers with his knees and then sets the pole height before beginning to hoist. The crew clips the pole to the mast eye and the helm completes the hoist. Finally the crew sets the guy and cleats it.

Retrieving to spinnaker chute
The crew makes sure that the downhaul is running freely (i.e. not snagged on the forestay or front of boat). The helm - steering with his knees - takes in all the slack on the downhaul before uncleating and, keeping hold of, the halyard, maintains some tension on this whilst beginning to pull in the downhaul. The crew maintains tension on the sheet. Once the centre (downhaul patch) of spinnaker has reached the chute, the crew unclips the pole from the mast and continues to hold on to it and the sheet while the helm pulls on the downhaul. Once most of the spinnaker is in the chute, the crew uncleats the pole from the guy, ensures the spinnaker clews have disappear into the chute and that the guy and sheet are cleated. The crew tidies up. In big waves in particular, it is important to ensure that the sheet and guy stay tidy and cleated to avoid them being snagged by a wave and pulling the spinnaker out of the boat. Crew and helm must communicate throughout the whole process to make sure they are not working against each other. When dropping the spinnaker from a tight reach in big winds, it can be more difficult for the helm to move into the centre of the boat. It helps to bear well away for the drop, and for the crew to help pull in the downhaul, particularly on a starboard reach because the helm is further away from the line of pull - the spinnaker being rigged on the port side.

Spinnaker trimming
It is important with the spinnaker to get the sail as flat as possible, which keeps the angle of attack shallow as well as opening the leech to leeward to stop the mainsail back-winding. To achieve this it is necessary to control the sheeting and pole position. The way to find the best pole height for the spinnaker is to hoist the sail, clip the pole onto the windward sheet and slide it forward until it touches the spinnaker clew. Now raise the pole at the outer end by pulling on the uphaul until a vertical crease appears from the centre of the head. This means that the sail is too flat and the edges have overtaken the middle. Then lower the pole to re-tension the leeches just enough to make the crease disappear. That is then as flat as that spinnaker will ever set. In fact it will be rather too flat for light winds, especially when running. Then more leech tension is needed to hold the air in and to keep the sail flying. In those conditions therefore, lower the pole a touch further. You should find that the outer edge of the pole needs to be 230-460mm above the horizontal. The next priority is to set the correct pole angle in relation to the wind, which is controlled by the guy. The pole should be just off the jib luff when sailing on a beam/close reach, in order to ensure that the pole is not damaged, particularly when sailing in strong winds. On a broad reach the pole will need to be positioned somewhere near an angle of 45 degrees back from the beam reach position. When running, the pole will be sufficiently far back to set the two clews to be at right angles to the wind. A rough guide is to set the pole at right angles to the wind,

SAILING FAST & EFFECTIVELY

Once the guy has been set, it is important to trim the spinnaker sheet continually, so that the windward luff is always on the point of slightly curling. Any adjustment should be gentle and an aggressive movement will tend to detach the air from the sail, causing it to collapse. The aim when trimming the spinnaker is to make the slot between this sail and mainsail as wide as possible and thereby generate as much forward power as can be achieved. Over-tightening the spinnaker leech congests the slot between it and the mainsail and the force from the spinnaker is then exerted at right angles to the "keel", contributing little to speed but a lot to heeling! Over-sheeting is in fact a major problem when flying a spinnaker. Fearful of wrathful comments from their helmsman, many crews will over-sheet the spinnaker, simply to stop it from collapsing. What they should be doing in fact, is just keeping the leading edge from collapsing, just so that it is on the verge of curling back at approximately half height. In other words, the object is not to pull the sheets, but rather the reverse, to keep easing and easing. The crew should be trying to get the clews as far away from the boat as possible. Don't worry about getting the two clews at the same height, except perhaps on a run (when it comes almost automatically). So, if the spinnaker doesn't collapse on a reach at least once, then it has been over-sheeted and is being kept too close to the other sails. Since the helmsman is constantly altering course to make the most of wind and waves, the crew will have to play the spinnaker all the time. The helm may be able to help with an occasional pull on the windward side. It is helpful to mark the sheets - the windward part of the sheet should be marked at one of the cleats so that the pole sets just off the forestay. Another mark, on the leeward part, will help in pre-cleating the spinnaker for a close reach. These marks are helpful in keeping the pole off the forestay and the spinnaker leech from being overtightened.

Beam reaching in breezier conditions

As the wind gets up on beam reach courses it is possible to get overpowered quite quickly and get into a stalled situation – heeled over, spinnaker flapping and going slowly with lots of leeway. In these conditions, ensure the kicker is freed off a bit to allow the wind to flow over the sail; bear off below the course and get the boat flat and planing fast, using the waves and keeping the spinnaker sheet eased as much possible. Raising the spinnaker pole helps to keep the top of the spinnaker flat. If still over-powered, the kicker can be freed right off so the mainsail is feathering at the top – yet further mainsail flattening can be achieved by pulling the cunningham in tight. The centreboard can be surprisingly well up, thus reducing the heeling moment – when travelling fast leeway isn't such a big issue! Once the boat is sailing fast and flat in its lovely stable planing mode, it will be relatively easy to get back on course, especially in lulls between the gusts. The gains to be made by freeing off fast with the spinnaker more than compensate for pointing up first without the spinnaker and trying to set it later - after everyone else has surfed past. There is always the option of taking the spinnaker down early in order to close reach up to the mark. Spinnaker trimming together with gybing, discussed below, respond enormously to practise and add immensely to the satisfaction of Wayfarer racing.

Reaching in breezier conditions - the mainsheet and kicker are well eased and there is some cunningham on. This allows the spinnaker - eased as much as possible - to keep pulling and maintain a well balanced helm

Gybing from one reach to another

It is essential to have a routine that is practised beforehand and is always adhered to. Think for a moment about what is involved: we want to alter the boat's course, to get all three sails from one side to the other and we want to change sides ourselves. All this without having to swim. If each job is given a number, then a proper sequence emerges:

1. Approach the mark well to windward. Give it a wide berth.

2. Look for suitable waves to gybe on, at the same time as looking for gusts. Do not attempt to gybe while decelerating in a wave or as the wind increases. Both slow the boat down relative to the wind and increase pressure on the sails. Arrange to gybe while accelerating or when the wind pressure on the sails is dropping.

3. As you approach the gybe point, the crew stands. He eases the leeward sheet and cleats it at the 'reach' mark for the other side. As he does so, the boat is borne away on to a dead run and the helm stands.

4. At this point the crew pulls the spinnaker around by pulling on the old windward sheet.

5. The main boom is sheeted in a bit, and, on order, the gybe is started, and the boom is flicked across by the helm.

6. As the crew goes over with the helm, he uncleats the jib, and takes the sheet from the other side with him.

7. The crew balances the boat, forgetting the sails until the boat is stable again.

8. The crew cleats the jib. On the order "NOW", from the helm, he goes forward to unclip the pole from the mast.

9. The leeward sheet is pulled out of the piston.

10. The uphaul is reorganised in its pole fitting if necessary.

11. The new windward sheet is fed through the pole end and that end is pushed forwards.

12. If the crew has cleated it right, before the gybe, the new windward sheet will stop the pole just short of the forestay, while the new leeward sheet, if pre-cleated correctly, should just enable the sail to set.

13. All this time, the helmsman should be refraining from such unhelpful comments as "Hurry up!" etc. He should be standing, balancing the boat for the straining, un-balanced crew and keeping the boat as upright as possible.

14. Be careful when feeding the windward sheet through the reaching hook near the shroud, or tensioning the windward barber hauler. This will bring the pole aft by tightening the windward sheet, and may cause the spinnaker to collapse.

15. The crew sits down, sheeting the jib in properly - easing or tensioning as necessary. Then he picks up the leeward spinnaker sheet.

16. The helmsman sheets in and off they go!.

Putting it all together around a course
This routine assumes a typical buoys-to-port, triangle-sausage-windward course and spinnaker bag launching:

(a) Before the start:
1. Carefully pack the spinnaker in port-side bag, ready to hoist without twists.

2. Cleat the port spinnaker sheet at its marked reach position.

3. Stow the pole on the starboard side of boom.

(b) Near the windward mark - at end of last port tack:
1. Unhook the spinnaker halyard from storage hook.

2. Make sure the port barber hauler is uncleated.

3. Feed one metre of starboard spinnaker clew out of the spinnaker bag and onto foredeck while tightening and cleating the starboard barber hauler from the port side of the boat.

At end of the last starboard tack:
1. If practical, the helm presets pole to correct sailing height.
2. Adjust controls for upcoming reach (e.g. outhaul, cunningham, kicking strap).

If practical it might be possible for the crew to get the pole up before the rounding as above. Note the spinnaker has been pulled out a bit onto the foredeck ready.......

...... usually the spinnaker pole goes up after the rounding

(c) After the rounding:
1. Check that it is tactically desirable to hoist - make sure that you will not be luffed or passed to windward.

2. When conditions are "go", the crew balances the boat while the helm hoists the spinnaker. This is especially important when the boat is (or may be) overpowered. The crew may regularly have to pull the jib in briefly after the hoist in order to free the spinnaker sheet, which sometimes catches under the jib foot. After this, the crew cleats the jib in an effective reaching position.

3. Once the halyard is carefully cleated, the helm takes over balancing duties while the crew sets the pole.

4. Once the pole is set, the spinnaker should fill since its sheet was pre-cleated. The crew then takes over the sheet and fine-tunes the spinnaker.

(d) At the gybe mark:
The approach:
As the helm begins to bear away for the gybe, the crew yanks the pole well aft to bring most of the spinnaker to the starboard side while releasing the leeward spinnaker sheet, cleats in the port barber hauler, and uncleats the jib – the helm waits until the crew is done before completing the gybe.

The gybe:
1. Both the helm and crew concentrate all energies on the gybe - the spinnaker, with both barber haulers cleated in should present no problem unless the gybe is badly mishandled - see page 29 for more details.

2. In windy weather, the crew helps the boom over by grabbing the kicking strap and exerting some pull on it without actually trying to force the boom over until it indicates it wants to go when the pressure on the sail decreases significantly. If a capsize is feared, the helm must do an S-gybe (i.e. pull the tiller briefly to port as the boom goes over).

After the gybe:
1. Helm & crew balance the boat and steer as tactics dictate (e.g. go high to defend wind) while trimming the main and jib to best effect.

2. The crew then completes the pole transfer while the helm drives and balances the boat. The crew uncleats the leeward barber hauler and sheets in.

(e) End of second reach - approaching the leeward mark:
1. The helm and crew set sail controls and board for the upcoming beat.

2. At word from the helm, the crew stands in front of the windward jib sheet and stows the pole. The helm may adjust the uphaul for storage parallel to the boom, or do it later, as the situation dictates.

3. The helm stands (briefly, if necessary!) to uncleat the spinnaker halyard and holds it in a light grip over his head to anticipate (and prevent) tangles. In a blow, the halyard can be thrown overboard to achieve the same effect.

4. The crew quickly pulls the spinnaker down while the helm exerts enough halyard pressure to prevent the sail from coming down faster than the crew can handle. If done quickly enough, there should be no risk of the leeward spinnaker sheet going under the boat - which is slow! (To prevent this, fix a 100mm stainless steel wire loop out from the bow.) The crew pulls all the slack from the spinnaker halyard and stows it around the storage hook near the shrouds.

Ready for the spinnaker drop - the helm holds the halyard lightly above head-height to anticipate any tangles!

At the leeward mark:
Having the board full down, playing the jib and keeping the boat flat as we round onto the beat are the priorities. Tidying up can be done later, when you're settled away on a tack that you expect to hold for a while.

(f) End of the second beat and start of the run:
1. Since the next leg will be a run, both barber haulers may want to be cleated in, but the windward one for sure!

2. Here the helm and crew can both work on the spinnaker at the same time: the helm hoists and then takes both sheets to fly the spinnaker while the crew fixes the pole. The crew needs to add the pole carefully so that the spinnaker, being so masterfully flown by the helm, will not be made to collapse!

3. Once the pole is attached, the helm can cleat the windward sheet in an appropriate position while the crew takes over the sheet. Coordinating their movements, helm sits/stands to leeward, crew to windward. In light airs, the helm holds the boom out and gives boat a windward heel to help the spinnaker set better.

(g) Run-to-run gybe:
Gybing on the run uses very similar techniques to reach to reach gybing, see Page 29, except that the crew should hand the sheets to the helm after gybing the main. The helm can then keep the spinnaker flying whilst steering with the tiller between his legs.

RACE TACTICS & STRATEGIES

You want to go faster – to raise your sailing skills – to race? How do you go about it? Obviously it is best to start at your home club, but hopefully as your skills improve, so will your ambition and desire to try events further afield. Apart from the pleasure and excitement of sailing in new waters, regardless of your final placing, what you will remember will be the enthusiasm and friendship of other members of the class fleet, and the encouragement engendered by racing together. The class magazines, website and forum tell you about many of the events planned throughout the country to help you make your choice of what to do and where to go.

The approach to racing strategy and tactics is basically the same whether you are entering the local regatta or one of the Wayfarer Class Championships. So the following articles are arranged to help you and your crew prepare yourselves and your boat, and take you through a race or a regatta from the time you have decided to enter until you finish, hopefully at sometime on the prize-winners' podium! Remember though, not everyone can be a champion immediately, so always set yourself an achievable objective; after all, finishing ahead of your peers in the boat park is sometimes just as satisfying.

RACING TIPS FROM MICHAEL McNAMARA

Pre-start warm-up

Picture the scene. It is a few seconds after the start. The smoke from the starting gun has barely left the transom of the committee boat. Stretching away down the line is a seemingly endless stream of boats all beating hard in unison. Yet is it as beautifully simple as that? Look at the detail. Then it is apparent that it is only the front-runners who are working hard. Behind them are a second and even a third rank of slower, wallowing boats already falling behind.

So, why are these boats behind? They may be in dirty wind and are having to plough through confused wash, but that is not enough. To see why, we have to go back a bit, before the start, back even beyond the warning signal. These were (probably) the boats sailing aimlessly about not doing their warm-up exercises. Not the sort of warm-up necessary in athletic sports although there are some who say sailors should warm up their muscle groups before the race. No, the warm-up we mean here is getting used to the conditions, so that both the crew and boat are in sync with their environment and can give it their all from the start. This will involve going through a series of small tasks:

1. By sailing hard on the wind on each tack for a few minutes it is pretty usual to note how the boat's heading alters as the wind shifts etc. However, this routine should also be used to get into the rhythm of the waves and wind. The sailors should be working hard at 'feeling' what the boat is telling them, of course. They could even take it in turns to close their eyes to use other senses – but the other should keep a good look out!

2. There should be lots and lots of tacking, feeling how the boat is affected by the waves. Here we are trying to find out what effect they have on the boat and how long it takes to get going again if we stop. Because gybing is (usually) not needed until later in the race it is not quite so critical but nonetheless a good few should be tried.

3. Acceleration is everything at the start. So, stop the boat and then see how long it takes to get going back up to full speed. This obviously varies with the conditions. If it is difficult to judge then use a mark as a fixed point.

4. If we are early at the start, we may need to stop. How can we do this? Practise letting the sails out, backing the sails aft; luffing-up (and therefore over the line) is not a good option. Then see how long it takes to get going and what is the best way of doing it. Work at sheeting the sails and at heeling angles etc.

5. By this time the line should be laid. So, which is the best end to start? Work it out and then go and make a few starts there just to see.

6. Practise your run up to the line seeing how long it takes and the effect of waves etc., but remember the actual start will have more boats about and so that the time getting there will be slower. Whilst doing all these, keep a really good look out all around. It would be a great shame to damage your boat or, even worse, to damage someone else's because you were concentrating too hard on other things. Going through this routine gives you the confidence to go into the start knowing that you can spring into action instantly because you know what is going to happen.

Michael McNamara takes a look at the pack while executing a perfect roll tack - European Championships, Holland 2006

Check the boat for example...	Rudder fittings are not slack - be careful about over tightening bolts holding them on to the transom.
	All shackles should be done up nice and tight - especially on the boom.
	Is the spinnaker pole on board and are the ends working?
	Are the bailers tight to the hull when up and is there any grit or sand in them?
	Have you a sponge and/or plastic bailer? Not Mk IV!
	Is the tiller extension secure? Check universal joint fastenings.
	Do all cleats etc., work?
	Have you a protest flag? (Not required under ISAF Rules, but may still be a requirement under the Sailing Instructions.)
	Do you have your tally if needed?
	What about food and drink?
Know the Sailing Instructions	If in doubt - ask.
	What about recall signals and general recall signals?
	How can the course be shortened?
	Will the finish be outside the course or on the last leg, does the windward mark have to be left on a required side?
Know the Course	What is the weather forecast?
	What about the tide? Do you know the time the tide will turn, the direction and strength of the current and the variations across the course?
	Can the land affect the wind?

RACE TACTICS & STRATEGIES

Starting

Sweaty hands; racing heart; shortness of breath; weakness in muscles... sounds familiar? Of course it does. Rather, it will do to every dinghy-racing helm. As those last few seconds to the start tick away – taking an eternity – we are assailed by all sorts of emotions. There's hope, of course, anticipation; even fear perhaps. They are all in there squirming away trying to drive us over the edge into ... raw panic! That is the panic that causes us to oversheet; to pinch; to heel over; to stop; to forget our acceleration routines... in short that causes us to make a bad start. Yet we should not feel like condemned people about to be shot. We should be able to control our destinies. All we need to do is follow the Golden Rules... they are obviously not foolproof, but they go a long way towards keeping things cool.

1. As those seconds tick away there is nothing that we can do about our position on the line. That was taken care of long ago when we went through our 'checking which is the right end to start' routines. In fact, there are quite a few ways to find out which is the best end. The most simple and therefore the easiest one, is to sail along the line, sheeting the mainsail in as perfectly as possible. Once you have got that organised, tack, but be careful not to alter the mainsail setting as you do so. As you sail away back down the line, check to see if the mainsail is set as perfectly as it was before. If it is not, then one or other end of the line is the paying end. So, if the mainsheet has to be eased the wind is further behind and so the end you are sailing from is the paying end. If the mainsheet has to be pulled in the wind is further in front and so the end you are sailing towards is the paying end. If the wind is shifting, you will have to check and keep checking, so don't sail outside the end of the line because it may be impossible to get right back to the end if the wind changes.

2. If it is obvious to you which is the paying end, then it will be obvious to everyone else. That leads to the fleet all ganging up together in one place. The result of this congestion is that the wind drops as it goes up and over the top of the mass, wash increases and confuses the wave pattern and, worst of all, boats congregate early and as they stop they raft up. If the committee boat is big, you can even run out of wind under it. So, to our cost, it is only one or two boats maximum that will get away. The rest will all wallow in their dirty wind. Much better to be just away from the paying end. To leeward of the bunch at the windward end, for example, with all the luffing rights etc. that gives you. Hidden from the race officer's eyes, you can nibble up to the line, and be ready to bear away, accelerate and go as soon as the gun goes. So, you have lost a few metres by being further down the line, but at least you are safe. Besides, the raft of boats to windward acts as a buffer against those poor unfortunate naive sailors who come down from the committee boat hoping to find space. If it is the leeward end that pays, then this playing for safety is even more important. The timing to get it right has to be so perfect that it is just not worth the risk to start right next to the buoy.

3. Never go outside the windward end of the line. As windward boat you have no rights. The Section C Mark Room rules do not apply at a starting mark surrounded by navigable water. Besides which, as you bear away hoping for a gap it will already be closed and you are speeding up to a certain 720 degree or worse.

4. Try to keep speed on. If you have to hover, do so a few seconds away from the line. Then you have got a chance to build up speed before the hordes envelop you; and envelop you they surely will if you try to hover exactly on the line. You will already have worked out how long it takes to get going in the conditions; so that is your guide to the safe hovering distance.

5. Practice your acceleration techniques and keep the boat upright; otherwise you will be in the dirty wind of the boat to leeward. When accelerating away, the correct technique is to sheet both sails in together in a smooth, non-jerking way. This will keep the boat tracking without it luffing-up and stopping. The rudder must not be used until the boat is moving, otherwise it acts as a brake. Try to bear away as the gun goes to get a bit of speed. You can only really do this if, as you nibbled to the line, you luffed-up minutely from time to time to create a gap between you and the boat to leeward. Do not overdo this, otherwise the gap will be spotted and will be filled by a boat coming in from behind, which then has rights over you because you are the windward boat! How unfair can you get?

6. As the fleet comes up to the start the wind will drop all the way down the line. So ease kickers; do not oversheet jibs; do not sit too far forward (or aft). Then as the fleet spreads out bring the controls back on to their proper settings.

7. Keep a good watch out all around and get your crew to do the same, reporting in all the time. Crews should be doing the timing too. In big fleets do not expect to hear the gun. There will be too much other noise and besides it is visual signals that count.

8. Do not try to tack too soon around the front of the committee boat. His anchor warp is dangling there desperate to entangle you. So, in your pre-start checks have a look at the anchor cables at both ends.

9. If you have made a really good start do not blow it in the euphoria of the moment. Relax and get on with the race, but a small smile is permitted! If you have blown the start don't panic - be consoled that everyone does from time to time, but you do not have to make a habit of it. Just get on with things -getting into the tacking routine as you hunt for clear air, keeping the boat moving. It is possible to make a comeback; after all there is a whole race in front of you to do it... all it needs is patience. In club races, if you have the courage, try starting at the back just to experience the feeling. Then if it happens in big time stuff you will not get so grumpy.

10. My favourite routine is to sail along the line on port, towards the right end looking for a gap to tack in to. If you remember in Golden Rule No.5 there will be gaps created all the time. All you have to do is find them!

11. It was Paul Elvstrom who said that 'if you're not over the line once in every five races then you're not trying.' Well if that is your view too, be over the line in non-important races, but I bet that it will be the other way round. If all else fails, keep your cool. There is a whole lot of race left to go.

First Quarter of the Beat

Even though you may not have heard it because there was so much other noise, the starting gun has gone (at last) and you have a reason for being. You have to get to that first mark and need to shift into 'race mode' quickly. Decisions made or not made in the next few moments are critical, often deciding your finishing position. If you choose carefully you can lead the pack, whilst if you take the wrong option, you will be catapulted backwards through the fleet.

So, what are these choices? They are in fact pretty simple and revolve around:

1. *The need for clear air.*
2. *Making sure that the boat is up to speed.*
3. *Getting into 'sync' with the wind shifts.*
4. *Going the right way up the beat.*

How you implement these choices, and how you choose which is the most important at any given time, will depend upon what the wind strength is and how good a start was made.

Clear Air

The lighter the wind, the more important the need for clear air. Those who made good starts, perhaps because they started just away from the main concentration of boats, will make massive gains as they easily come up to speed. If they have space to leeward they can sail marginally freer to ease out in front. They are the lucky ones. So, what about those boats who did not get a good start? How do they get clear air? Well, the answer is that they must start hunting and hunting straight away. They will be in less wind so should ease kickers, sheet loads etc. They should not try to point. Foils do not start working until water flows over their surfaces. So a boat going slowly is a boat going sideways, falling into the dirty water of the boats to leeward. Go for the best speed you can. The majority of boats just after the start are on starboard. It will be impossible to break through to leeward of them. So, as soon as you can, tack. Tack sensibly and keep the boat moving. Panicky and awkward tacks only make things worse. Then take transom after transom, if necessary. You easily break through the dirty wind zone but do not forget to ease sails if you have to bear away.

Once an area of clear wind is found, begin thinking about the wind. Try to stay in touch with the shifts, deciding whether you have to go one way or the other up the beat. But keep looking to windward. If there is a flag pointing at you and you are within five to six mast lengths, then you are being covered. So, start hunting again. A word of warning. Do not tack so often that you lose speed. Better to be in dirty air for a moment while you get the boat moving. Then, when at a reasonable speed for the conditions, tack. Do not forget to look over your aft shoulder (especially when on starboard) just before you tack. There is nothing worse in this situation than having to tack twice in succession. If there is a boat there and it is too close, just bear away to create a gap (and speed) and then after tacking duck his stern.

Boat Speed

As you all know, boat speed is always important but perhaps not as essential in shifty conditions. It is only in steady winds that it really comes into its own. Remember that there is going to be much less wind and more of a confused sea in the congested start area. So as you approach the line you have to ease off from your pre-start settings – settings made in smoother sea and stronger winds. This rule applies even to the front markers, because the wind lifts away from the surface as it approaches the massed fleet. Then as the fleet spreads out, start to increase the loadings again. Take extra special care to keep the boat level, as heeling forces your sails into the backwind of leeward boats. Watch out for fore and aft trim, perhaps sitting slightly forward in the lighter airs and moving aft as the fleet spreads out. Remember to monitor speed constantly by comparing yourself with other boats. The golden rules are: make leeches tighter (without flattening sails) to improve pointing; open leeches and flatten sails to get more speed.

Getting into 'sync' with wind shifts

Most of the sailing you do is in shifty conditions where the wind oscillates about the mean, so as you clear the line begin using information learnt in pre-race practices. What is the wind doing compared to the mean? Is the wind heading or lifting? If you are on a significant header, tack if you can even if it means ducking a few sterns and losing some ground in the short term. You will be ahead of the boats you had to duck when the wind heads back and you will tack again on the new lift. If you cannot tack, do not worry too much. Just sail through the header, take the next lift and then wait for the next header before going. Easy to say but much harder to do. What usually happens is that you spot the header but cannot tack because of boats on your windward quarter. You start to fret and as your sailing goes down the tubes the situation is made much worse than it really is. A much better solution would be to shrug your shoulders (leave the fretting to others) and cope with what you have got.

Going the Right Way

Perhaps more accurately this should be entitled 'Getting ready to go the Right Way'. In fact, this is often overlooked in the urgency of a short-term gain. For example, in a gently bending breeze, many sailors hang on and hang on to the outside of the bend rather than tack and duck transoms. However, as it will pay to get on the inside of this wind bend, it is vital to tack onto the (apparent) header, again ducking sterns if necessary.

Remember that because you are sailing into the bend, you will soon be ahead of everyone you duck. The same tactics interestingly enough should be adopted in tidal situations where the need to get out of (or into) the current overcomes virtually everything else.

Insisting on your starboard rights and forcing port tack boats on to your lee bow is absolutely ridiculous if you are going the right way. Just think how you will feel as you are forced to tack away to clear your wind. By the same token always duck the starboard boat if you are on port and going the right way. In either case, however, if you are on the wrong tack, try your hardest to force the other boat away. The port tacker will have to be made to lee bow you so that you can tack off. The starboard tacker will have to be lee bowed vigorously to force him to tack. If in doubt, take the tack that will take the boat closest to the windward mark. Check tidal/current flow, and always try to get a lee bow if there is the merest chance. Keep a constant watch to windward, watching out for signs of likely changes in either wind strength or direction - smoke, other boats, etc. In light winds, keep the boat moving and do not keep tacking and tacking. In a breeze, watch the approaching waves. Whatever happens, they must not stop the boat. So, if necessary, ease the sheets, bear away and accelerate.

It is a pretty demanding time for you all, but if you get it right, the rewards are enormous. You will be ahead of the pack and able to move without pressure on to the next stage – the rest of the first beat including that oh so important final approach to the windward mark.

Sailing to Windward

Sailing to windward even in normal conditions is hard and demanding. When you have to do it in a breeze it becomes exhausting and in light weather, when that windward mark just refuses to get any closer, it becomes very, very frustrating. When you compare all that hard work with the glamour, thrills and sheer exhilaration of three sail spinnaker reaching, then it makes one wonder whether beating is worth all the effort. Of course it is ... it even has its own strange fascination. The aim, of course, is to make the beat as short and quick as possible. The speed made good to windward is, in fact, a compromise between sailing as close as possible to the wind (pointing) and sailing as fast as possible through the water (footing). Some sailors have the knack to do this right from the word go. Understanding that, they need constantly to trade the importance of one against the other, depending on what is demanded. Sometimes pointing high at the expense of speed and sometimes sailing rather lower, to go for extra speed at the expense of pointing. This perhaps, can best be described as having the 'feel' of the boat. For those sailors who have to work at getting this feel there are certain invaluable guides to help them:

Windtufts (Telltales)

When the sail is working properly, all three windward tufts will stream upwards at approximately 45 degrees. The leeward windtufts will be parallel to the water. If the top windward windtuft collapses first, the leech is too slack. The solution is to sheet in slightly. If the bottom windward windtuft collapses first, then the leech is too tight, so ease the sheet slightly. Once all three are working together, then the helm can modify the heading angle depending on what the helm wants to do, knowing that the leading edge of the sail is presenting a constant angle to the wind. If helms want to go for speed, they can bear away just enough to get the windward tufts parallel to the water, being careful of course, not to bear away so far that the leeward tufts collapse or that the wind coming from further abeam causes too much heeling over! If helms want to pinch a bit, they can feather up until the windward tufts go vertical or even flow towards the luff. Here they have to be careful not to luff up so far that the airflow breaks down and the tufts collapse.

Sometimes it is difficult to get the bottom windward and leeward tufts in sync. First the windward one goes and then immediately the leeward one collapses. This usually means that the leading edge is too straight and the wind finds it too easy to go from one side to the other. Slacken the rig tension slightly to give a touch of jib luff sag. You may not point so high, but you will go a lot quicker.

Steering

There is a nice simple rule to steering upwind. The helm is constantly moving of course, to keep the boat on track, but if the crew can feel the boat altering course then it is too violent. Some say that you have to steer through or around waves, but this is hard to do accurately, so for most sailors it pays to let the boat have its track and let the waves do their worst. However, if the boat hits two or three waves in succession then bear away a bit, ease the sheets and get some speed before heading up again. Do not confuse 'feel' with the tug of weather helm. Weather helm is the boat telling you that it's in trouble and needs help. It's probably heeling too much or the mainsail leech is too tight. Easing the main slightly and heading up minutely are often the answer. In most conditions, therefore, a neutral helm is the fastest. Unfortunately, it is also the most difficult to get used to.

Wash

Checking the wash is a good guide to speed. The smoother, the faster, is the golden rule. In light weather, watch out for that leeward aft chine digging in. This shows up as a curling, turbulent wavelet to leeward off the rudder wash. Don't forget to sit back in a breeze to get the flatter, more powerful after sections in the water and the veed bow out. Obviously the sailors have to move forward in lighter winds to get that transom out.

Anticipation

As sailors, we have to develop split personalities, as part of us has to deal with the here and now – coping with what the wind and waves are doing to the boat at that particular moment. At the same time, a part of us has to keep looking ahead to see what is about to happen. Will the next gust be a header of a freer? Will this wave stop the boat? And so on. This is where the crew can help and both sailors, by looking to windward, can make their judgement as to what to do. Crews should be especially encouraged to give their views. This means that there should be plenty of chat about where the gust is and what it will do etc. Even if the sailors are totally wrong, it doesn't matter. At least they know that the gust is coming and interestingly after a while the gusts start to agree with you!

Avoid the Lay Lines

If your final approach for the windward mark is made too far out then you are liable to experience the wind direction changing, which you can't take advantage of, as you are locked into the tack; or some rotten sailor coming across in front and tacking on you. So you have to tack and sail much further than you should!

The Approach to the Windward Mark

This is often when many places are lost and gained. As boats start to converge, the wave turbulence increases and the wind becomes more chopped up. So avoid getting to leeward of other boats if you can, even if it means sailing out beyond the lay line slightly. The extra distance sailed is more than made up by the extra speed. Avoid approaching the mark on port if you can. There may be a gap in the starboard horde but more usually there isn't! So, remember, the faster you do the beat, the quicker you get on to those lovely reaching legs – but first of all we have to round the mark…..

Rounding Marks

Don't you dare hit it. When rounding on its windward side in windy conditions, leave a good boom's length to spare. In rough conditions with big waves, the mark will be moving about quite a lot, so keep well away. When approaching any mark, check which way the tide or current, if any, is flowing. The buoy could be leaning away from the current and there might be a wake. The general rule of thumb is to approach the mark wide and leave it close. This stops others from barging in. Try to keep mark rounding simple by not tacking too close either before or after the mark. In other words, sailors should try to settle down, both in approaching and in leaving the mark. As they are approaching a mark, both sailors should know where the next mark is, and what sort of a leg it will be getting there, i.e. how the sails, etc. are likely to be controlled.

Reaching

But are they so prepared? Preparation for the reaching legs is often the last thing on most sailors' minds as they finally get to the windward mark. In windy weather they are often too exhausted to care, whilst in light airs they can be too frustrated at the time it has taken getting up the beat. Add to these negative feelings the anarchy that reigns in the middle of large fleets, and it becomes almost irrelevant where the gybe mark is. As Billy Bacon once said 'Blow where the next mark is, where is this one?' However, assuming that the mark was rounded without being hit, it is then and only then, that those sailors who haven't planned ahead start to get ready for the reach. For many it is then just in that relaxed moment, as the boom end clears the mark, that disaster so often strikes. The crew dives in from the weather gunwale to do all those things to get the boat ready for the reach. Kicker, cunningham, clew outhaul and centreboard all apparently have to be eased, and what is more, they have to be done in microseconds of rounding the mark. So what happens? The helm, alarmed at the boat heeling (at this stage the boom may be in the water) tries to bear away and ease the mainsheet. The boat, on the other hand, is trying to broach as it builds up an impressive leeward bow wave. All of which results in a slow agonising wipe out. Important as all that energetic unloading of tension is, it must take poor second place to the primary purpose of any reaching leg.

The main purpose of the reaching leg is to consolidate your position on the boats that are attacking you, whilst at the same time trying to gain on the boats in front. The name of the game is 'not to lose places'. So, rounding a mark in a breeze should mean both sailors staying on the windward side. This actually helps the boat to bear away by creating a slight heel to windward, and creating a weather bow wave (do not take this effect too far or the results will be spectacular). If there are waves about, then that is the time to catch one. It's one of life's great unsolved mysteries as to why the best waves are always near the windward mark! Do not look behind, do not worry about the detail, drive the boat down the face of the wave keeping the boat balanced. Your sole purpose in life is to stretch the distance between you and your attackers.

After the wave has finished with you and the crew can safely move in without heeling the boat, all the usual jobs can be done! Of course this is an ideal situation and is usually reserved for those who round the windward mark clear of other boats. It is perhaps only those lucky few up with the leaders who have that sort of space – is it any wonder they gain! However, for the rest of us, there are some general rules, which govern tactics as you bear away around the windward mark; if you are leading a pack then stay fairly high to stop the opposition driving over the top of you. Remember that once one gets your wind, the rest are as good as past. If you are following a gang away from the mark, then go low; do not get drawn into a luffing match and aim to gain an overlap for the gybe mark.

Having laid down these general rules, there are of course, other factors to take into account: be very wary of going too high if the tidal current is setting to windward and/or if the leg is likely to become even broader. The tactic here is that after defending your position; work down little by little to the rhumb line as soon as possible, taking a transit on the mark from time to time. Do not go low if the tidal current is setting you to leeward or if the wind is forward of the beam, especially if it is too strong for you to handle comfortably. It is no wonder that in big fleets the classic reaching chevron is very soon achieved, as boats try to stay out of the wake of the boat ahead and either go to leeward to try for the overlap or go to windward to try to steal the wind. As boats get further from the windward mark the more they spread out, and therefore the easier it is to get free wind. So, if you have opted for the windward course, do try to get back down again in nice easy stages bit by bit. If you leave it to the last moment to bear away, then the slower you go and the easier it is for the other leeward boats to get water. Clear air is a major concern all the way down the reach, so keep looking at the (inevitable) gang of boats around you and make sure that their pennants are not aiming at you – especially if you are within four boat lengths. Also, try to avoid the confused wash of the boats in front. This is especially important in planing or surfing conditions when it is vital to get into the rhythm of the waves.

The knack of course, is not to look at the wave you are about to use, but the back of the one that has just left you. With the bow in the trough, between the two, the sailor will feel the windward quarter start to lift. If possible they should almost anticipate its lift by moving to windward to keep the boat upright. If it is allowed to heel, even by the merest amount, speed will be lost and the boat will not want to bear away. If sailors overdo it a bit and the boat heels to windward, that doesn't matter, because it helps the boat bear away down the face of the wave without using that rudder/brake thing at the back! The track of a boat surfing down the face of the wave will not usually be along its keel line. It will be more crab-like and at an angle. This skidding is best achieved by raising the centreboard rather more than you would think normal. The helm will be able to feel when the board is raised too much as 'helm' comes on and there is also a curved vortex wave on the windward side of the rudder wake. So, drop the board an inch or two and that's just about right. By the way, if the board is raised too much, you have plenty of time to think about it as you swim around the boat to climb back on it! However, the motto is 'if the board is in the box, water and its attendant weight and turbulence are not'. As the gybe mark approaches, boats start to converge again, making the problems of getting free air and smooth water even more acute. As the gybe mark gets closer, think ahead. Keep saying to yourself 'where do I want to be when I round the mark?' The longer the preparation time, the better the chance of getting it right.

Running

Getting down the run is a compromise between sailing the shortest distance on a dead run and luffing up slightly to build up extra speed. The general rule is that it pays to luff up to keep moving in very light winds, or to get the boat planing in marginal planing conditions. As soon as the boat planes, it pays to start bearing away again. The problem is, of course, that luffing up increases distance sailed and so the extra speed has to at least compensate for the extra distance. As a general rule therefore, tacking downwind does not pay. Because of its heavy weight, the Wayfarer does not plane sufficiently fast downwind to make up for the extra distance sailed. If, sailing marks to port, you approached the windward mark on a starboard tack lift (or marks to starboard on a port tack lift), it will pay to gybe straightaway after rounding. If you approached the mark on a header instead, it will pay to leave the mark without gybing. Everything else being equal, consider on which side the spinnaker is stowed, as you decide on which gybe to choose. On a run, it is often easier to hoist the spinnaker on the windward side. Hoisting to leeward means that the spinnaker has to be pulled around the jib sheets, etc. When approaching a leeward mark, think about what side the spinnaker will be used on next. Try to get it stowed so that you will have a leeward hoist for an upcoming reach. Since the spinnaker should always be lowered to windward, you may need to do an extra gybe to achieve the desired effect.

Changing Gear

You are going well. The boat is flying and you are up with the pack. Then, quite suddenly, horribly, and often without apparently altering anything, it all changes. To leeward, boats point higher and go faster and the windward boats start to roll over. So, what has happened? Why are things going wrong and what can you do about it? DON'T PANIC. You were going well and can do so again, providing that you are logical. So, identify whether it is a pointing problem or a speed deficiency problem; then apply a checklist of cures. Do not forget to alter only one thing at a time and then give it a chance to work before going on to try the next.

So, you need to POINT HIGHER:

Q:	*Is the mainsail leech too open?*
A:	Try tightening it by:
	increasing mainsheet tension
or	increasing kicking strap tension
or	bring the boom closer to the centreline.

Use the angle of the top batten to the boom as your guide, ideally it should be parallel. The top windtuft should, in fact, be streaming aft most of the time, but stalling it, up to 40% of the time should give the best pointing ability, although at the expense of speed.

Q:	*Is the mainsail too flat?*
A:	straighten mast or ease clew outhaul

If the mainsail is too flat the leech is likely to be too open and the slot between the foresail leech and the front of the main too wide. A good guide here is that if the main luff does not backwind in medium conditions from time to time, then the mast is too bent. Also the sail can have large diagonal creases, which in extreme cases will flutter.

Q:	*Is the foresail too full at the luff?*
A:	increase rig tension
or	ease luff cunningham until luff has minute wrinkles
or	move fairlead closer to the centreline.

Identify this problem by luffing up rather more than usual to see if the whole luff length collapses at the same time. As increasing the rig tension straightens out the angle of attack, it is possible to go too far and make the sail difficult to 'read'.

Q:	*Is the foresail leech too open?*
A:	sheet foresail harder
or	move fairlead forward
or	reduce mast rake or increase jib halyard tension.

This problem shows itself when luffing up more than is usual. If the top windward windtuft collapses first, tensioning the foresail halyard reduces rake, raises the clew and so tensions the leech.

Q: *Is the helm too neutral and has no 'feel'?*
A: increase mast rake
or sit further forward
or angle centreboard forward

Some 'feel' is necessary to the helm in order to keep the boat on track when the helm is looking elsewhere. Up to 70% of windward concentration is spent in looking outside the boat in anticipating what changes in the environment are about to affect the beat. So, try one adjustment at a time, waiting a while to see if it makes an improvement.

So you want to go FASTER?

Q: *Is the mainsail too full?*
A: bend the mast more or tighten clew outhaul.

Aim to make the sail inert in the gusts, so that it feathers rather than flaps. In a breeze the very best speed seems to come when the top quarter of the sail has very little curve and will seem almost straight when viewed from below. The top telltale will stream all the time.

Q: *Is the mainsail leech too tight?*
A: increase mast bend
or ease boom away from centreline on mainsheet/bridle/traveller or tighten clew outhaul

A sign that the leech is too tight is excessive and uncontrollable heeling in gusts, and the boat tries to luff up viciously.

Q: *Is there excessive weather helm?*
A: keep boat level and do not allow to heel
or reduce rake
or move crew weight aft
or raise centreboard a fraction

This problem shows itself particularly in gusty conditions when the out-of-balance boat tries to luff into the wind as the gust hits. Keeping the boat flat and moving aft not only keeps the hull shape symmetrical but also makes better use of the fatter, flatter aft sections.

Q: *Is the foresail angle of attack too shallow?*
A: reduce halyard tension
or reduce rig tension overall
or tension foresail cunningham
or move fairlead outboard

If the angle of attack is shallow the sail is not only difficult to read but the centre of effort goes aft. When this happens, the bottom windtufts become unstable as first the windward one and then the leeward one stall out as the airflow fluctuates from one side to the other.

Q: *Is the foresail leech too tight?*
A: ease sheet slightly
or move fairlead aft slightly
or increase mast rake

This shows as excessive mainsail backwinding and the lower windward windtuft collapses before the top one. Aim to keep the middle leech parallel to the centreline with the leech at .75 height being 5–10% open and the leech at .25 height being 5–10% closed. Tiny movements of sheet and fairlead adjustment have massive effect on the leech so do not overdo them. So, as a general rule, flatter is faster, while a tighter leech improves pointing.

Weather for Racing

What is the weather about to do? We need to define what the term 'weather' actually means to us. To the sailor, of course, it invariably means WIND. Unfortunately even daily forecasts are not detailed enough to be of much use on the race course except that they provide valuable background information. This can be added to what we see happening on the course to enable us to make a best guess of what to do. In fact, we sailors need to know not only what the wind will be doing during the race but also more importantly what is going to happen to it on the leg we are on. This is never going to be a precise science and so we must not become too complicated or too obsessed in our analysis. Our forecast is really only one part of our overall race strategy as boat organisation, crew technique, boat-to-boat tactics all play their part too. Which of them has priority at any one time depends upon our immediate needs at that moment. Notwithstanding all that, getting to the first mark in a good position is often everything and usually decides our finishing position in that race. We therefore need to spend time thinking about our options and what is likely to be the best way up the beat. Later on in the race of course, we do not have the luxury of that spare time as so many other pressures are heaped on us. Now, although we can feel the wind we obviously cannot see it. Therefore we have to observe how it affects things around us – clouds; smoke; trees; other boats, etc. Our timetable on the countdown before the start should therefore be:

On the journey to the sailing club:

What is the wind forecast and are the clouds moving in the same direction as that forecast?

Could nearby landmasses affect the wind at the surface: Is the wind along the shore, or is it offshore or onshore?

Are conditions right for a sea breeze to develop (land heating up – gentle offshore breeze)?

Is the air stream stable (smooth cloud cover and hazy conditions) or is it unstable (cumulus clouds, clouds with jagged bases and good visibility)? Could it rain during the race?

What will the currents be doing?

Sailing to the Start
Note the wind direction and speed on a regular basis:
Is the cloud base lowering as we look to windward?
Is the current affecting the water (wave heights and tide lines perhaps)?

Preparation for the Start
We should sail as much of the beat as we can to check on gusts and lulls; on wind bends and the effect of shorelines etc., to decide what side is going to pay.

Up the first beat
If one side is paying we should make a mental note to go that way up the next beat if the environment stays the same.

So, what are we looking out for when we go through these routines?

1. The Weather Forecast and Gradient Winds
One of the reasons that weather forecasts are only a background help is that the wind they describe is the gradient wind. This is the wind at about 500 metres up and is high enough not to be affected by the surface. However, it is the wind on the surface that we use and it is obviously affected by surface friction. Not only is it generally weaker, but also it is twisted to the left. The technical term for wind going to the left i.e. against the sun's direction is 'backed'. If it goes to the right it veers as it follows the sun's direction. Over waters where friction is less the surface wind is backed by about 10 degrees. Overland with increased friction it can be as much as 40 degrees backed over the gradient wind.

2. Wind blowing Offshore
As the wind leaves the shore it will veer because of the change in surface friction. This gentle bend to the right can extend for some distance down wind. It can be spotted in our pre-race practice as we beat towards the shoreline checking our compass readings. The wind increases in strength as it leaves the shoreline behind and becomes more stable as the difference between the gusts and the lulls becomes less marked.

3. Wind blowing Onshore
There will be no changes in direction on the water as the shoreline approaches; almost invariably there will be less wind afloat than could be guessed at when standing on the shore.

4. Wind blowing along the Shore
With the coast on your right when standing with your back to the wind, the differing angles of the surface wind on the land and the water increase the wind strength just offshore as they merge together. With the coast on your left when standing with your back to the wind, this time the effect is the opposite as the two breezes separate and reduce wind strength for quite a distance offshore.

5. Gusts and Lulls
Gusts and lulls occur in unstable air and happen when the surface and gradient winds become mixed up. This overturning of the air occurs as air above the surface heats up and rises, often forming cumulus clouds as it does. It is replaced by cold air dragged down bringing the stronger winds from above. As they hit the water we see the typical darkening ripples. Interestingly these gusts occur between the clouds. Underneath the clouds the wind will be lighter because of the updraught. So, if at all possible, avoid sailing under them. So, when looking to windward, if there are more cumulus clouds on one side, head for the other side of the course.

6. Raining Clouds
These are usually darker than cumulus clouds. If rain is falling under a cloud then air is being cooled and so the air will be falling and the wind will be stronger. So, head for dark raining clouds.

7. Cloud base lowering to Windward
This means a front (junction between a warm and cold air mass) is approaching. Winds increase as the front gets closer. The appearance of the front is marked by heavy rain. Approach this on port, as the wind will have backed with the approach of the rain. As the cloud base rises behind the deluge, tack onto starboard because the wind will veer by as much as 90 degrees! In the unstable air stream afterwards, with lots of cumulus, the wind will become blustery and we are back into trying to stay away from the clouds!

8. Thunderstorms approaching with anvil shaped clouds
Obviously the forces creating this lot are pretty powerful. Air is forced upwards at an enormous rate. It is rapidly cooled and then blasts down to hit the water and fans out in very strong gusts. Hailstones only add to the misery!

9. Sea Breezes
Sea breezes occur when the air temperature over the land is higher than the air temperature over the sea. This usually happens on a sunny day as the heated air over the land rises and drags colder air in from the sea. The air over the land then flows out to sea and as it cools, falls to take the place of the air moving towards the shore. We can see the mechanism starting as cumulus clouds build over the land and clouds from the sea dissolve. As the sea breeze develops it turns gradually to the right, by as much as 50–60 degrees, by mid-afternoon. This breeze dies away during the evening.

10. Effect of Current
A current flowing against the wind increases the strength of the wind that the boat is using. It also increases friction between the wind and water and so waves become higher and steeper with shorter distances crest to crest. These waves could slow the boat down somewhat, so it may pay to try and find flatter water even though that means there will be less weather going current. Conversely current flowing with the wind reduces the strength of the wind the boat is using. Because friction between wind and water is reduced the water is flatter as the top of the wave is 'planed-off'. Pointing is poor in these circumstances and speed over the ground is very much reduced. It is a situation very much to be avoided if at all possible!

Protesting (and alternatives)

Penalty turns

Very few Wayfarer sailors practise 720° turns and yet they should. Imagine how tense the situation is! An incident has occurred. The sailor has admitted responsibility and must begin his turns as soon as he is clear of other boats. He's het up. Which way does he go? Luff up to tack or bear away to gybe? It invariably seems to pay to gybe first. Luffing up is far too slow, especially if the centreboard is not down.

Deciding whether to protest or not

So, you have been involved in an 'incident' out on the race course. Now you have to cope with it. Whatever else happens, do not lose your temper. Make up your mind very quickly whether you are in the right or not. The Racing Rules of Sailing (RRS) are designed to keep boats apart. Rule 14 'Avoiding Contact' states:-

'A boat shall avoid contact with another boat if reasonably possible. However, a right-of-way boat or one entitled to room or mark-room:

a) need not act to avoid contact until it is clear that the other boat is not keeping clear or giving room or mark-room,

b) shall not be penalised unless there is contact that causes damage or injury.'

If you think you are in the right then Rule 61.1 requires that you have to inform the other boat by hailing 'Protest' as this gives the other boat a chance to carry out 720° turns. If you know that you are in the wrong then either retire or accept an alternative penalty (if they are allowed under the Sailing Instructions). As soon as you have hailed 'Protest' forget about the incident until after the race, but make a note of nearby sail numbers, as you may need a witness later on. Get sailing again as quickly as possible and do not get involved in a shouting match. When you are ashore you should try to find the sailor you are protesting against and inform him that you intend to protest. Remember, he may not have heard your hail on the water.

Alternative Procedures

If an incident on the water is not resolved by a boat taking a penalty - one turn for touching a mark, two turns for breaking a rule of Part 2 of the Racing Rules of Sailing - then the outcomes have traditionally been: i) a protest hearing which may result in a disqualification; (ii) a boat retires after finishing; (iii) nothing happens, because there is no protest, and no retirement. However further possibilities have been developed in order to streamline the process:

(a) An Exoneration Penalty which is less severe than disqualification may be provided by the Sailing Instructions for many infringements. A 20% scoring penalty is recommended by the RYA as stated in rule 44.3(c). However, this can be varied in the sailing instructions according to the level of the event. For example, a 30% scoring penalty may be more appropriate at an Open Meeting, and a 40% scoring penalty at a National Championship. This penalty may be accepted after finishing and before the start of any protest hearing. Once it is accepted, a protest committee cannot penalise that boat further over the same incident; and neither can it be withdrawn even if a protest committee later decides no rule was broken.

(b) An Advisory Hearing is intended to be a new quicker way (than a protest committee) of resolving disputes. Its purpose is to discuss incidents with an adviser and resolve them promptly in an informal but positive way, so that competitors understand the rules better. It is available only where there is no injury or serious damage. When an Advisory Hearing is requested, and if all parties agree to this procedure, an adviser will quickly hear what the parties have to say, decide whether the issues are clear enough without further evidence, and, if so, say whether any boat broke a rule, stating which one and why. However if all else fails here are some guidelines on the protest procedure:

Filling out the protest form

Complete the Protest Form and hand it to the Race Committee (via the Beachmaster perhaps) before the end of the Protest time. If it is close to the end then get the time noted on the form. The form needs to be completed correctly. Rule 61.2 'Protest Contents' states that:-

'A protest shall be in writing and identify

a) the protester and protestee;
b) the incident, including where and when it occurred;
c) any rule the protester believes was broken; and
d) the name of the protestor's representative.

However, if requirement (b) is met, requirement (a) may be met at any time before the hearing, and requirements (c) and (d) may be met before or during the hearing.'

The form itself is straightforward to complete. It requires details of the protesting boat and of the boat being protested; the whereabouts and time of the incident; when the flag was flown; when an attempt to inform the protestee was made; as well as the number(s) of the Rule(s) considered infringed. Where many sailors come to grief is in the description of the incident. It is always best to make a rough copy on scrap paper first. In this description outline:

- *the build up to the incident including any verbal warnings given (e.g. 'water'; 'starboard' etc);*

- *the incident itself;*

- *what happened immediately afterwards.*

This outline should also be followed in the form of a diagram, being very careful to position the boats accurately and to scale. Make a drawing on scrap paper first. Remember to include reasonably accurate distances (i.e. 1½ boat lengths etc.) but be wary of being too pedantic (i.e. 49½ cm), as no one can be that accurate on the water. The Protest Committee have to base their decisions on what rules apply and who (if any) is to be disqualified on FACTS FOUND. The description and diagram are therefore important ammunition for the protester because they will be read before the hearing. They will provide the basis for the Protest Committee's understanding of what happened. So make it NEAT, CLEAR and PRECISE to show that you know what you are talking about. However, do not worry too much about making mistakes, say in the Rules, as you will be able to put it right later.

Are you being protested?
One problem that can occur if you are being protested is that you do not see the protest form until the hearing. This is wrong. It is against Rule 63.2. So, as soon as you know that you are being protested ask the Race Committee (perhaps via the Beachmaster) to let you see the protest form before the meeting, as you need a reasonable time to prepare a defence. This could include time to find witnesses. So, it is a good idea at the end of the protest time to look at the notice board to see if you are being protested.

Witnesses
Try and find witnesses to the incident. Find out what they saw and providing that their view is sympathetic to your cause, ask them to come to the protest meeting. There is often a reluctance to do this (for various reasons) so do not be too upset if they refuse. Some incidents such as the Tacking Rule, Rule 13, and the Mark-Room Rule, Rule 18 are very difficult to prove without witnesses. DO NOT ATTEMPT TO PUT WORDS INTO YOUR WITNESS'S MOUTH as this will come out badly at the meeting. It doesn't matter if your witness did not see it all precisely as it happened because these incidents happen so quickly.

The Protest Meeting
Find out where and when the protest meeting is and make sure that you and your witness are there early. Whilst waiting, do not enter into angry discussions with the opposition. As you will be present throughout the hearing, try to go to the loo beforehand. You do not want to have to leave halfway through and miss some vital information.

Handling your case
The way you handle your case at the meeting is very important. You must not be so over-confident that you irritate the Committee nor must you be so self-effacing that they cannot get the relevant information out of you! Do bear in mind that the members of the Committee may not know your class well and for example, they may be unsure of acceleration rates or how quickly the boat slows down. They may also be as nervous as you and may not even know the protest procedure or the RRS all that well and find the RRS Book hard to read. Sometimes, this nervousness comes out in a terse, almost hostile manner towards the two sailors. At the other extreme, some Protest Committees enjoy the whole procedure. They usually know the RRS well and have the off-putting habit of quoting a barrage of rule numbers. DO NOT LET EITHER SORT PUT YOU OFF.

Questions during the hearing
The Protest Committee are required to ask questions before starting the hearing. They will ask whether you object to any member of the Committee on the grounds of 'interest'. Be careful about objecting as this could alienate you but if you feel that you may not get a fair hearing (perhaps because they are relatives of the opposition) then say so. They can overrule your objections. They will also need to find out whether the requirements of Rule 61 have been carried out. Was the flag flown; was an attempt to notify the other boat made; is the protest form filled out in enough detail to identify the incident? If either of the first two were missed out they have no choice other than to reject the protest, even though there may have been a collision (Rule 63.5) You, as the protester, will then be asked to state your case. Remember, it is all about the 'finding facts' situation, so do not make it over-complicated. Organise your points so that 'finding facts' is easy for the Committee (e.g. 'I was on starboard' or, 'we were four hull lengths from the mark' etc). You will then be asked questions by the protestee and perhaps by the Committee, although they usually like to leave this until the protestee has made his case. Listen carefully while he does this. Does he differ? Where does he differ? How can you make it clear that his arguments do not describe the incident as it happened? Then, when invited, ask your questions that clarify the situation to your advantage (i.e. 'you stated that we were two hull lengths apart when you tacked, yet the collision took place thirty seconds after you had borne away on to a close hauled course. Surely those two do not tie up do they?' 'How far can a boat travel in thirty seconds?' and so on). The Committee will ask questions of both of you to clarify things in their own minds. So keep it simple and do not contradict yourself. Witnesses are then invited to state the position as they see it. Questions to them can be asked by both sailors and the Committee. If witnesses show you in a good light keep it short. If the opposition try to shoot them down, come back with supportive questions to bring out the good points again.

Finally, both you and the opposition will be asked to make a statement. Emphasise the points made in your original statement, modified perhaps by what the witnesses and the opposition said. Try to emphasise the good points and play down the opposition's arguments without being derogatory. That is it. When the protestee has made his own statement, you will be asked to withdraw. The Committee then have to find the relevant facts, and use them to judge which Rules apply and reach a decision... hopefully in your favour. Even if the verdict goes against you, accept it with good grace and shake hands with the opposition, if possible in front of the Committee. Win or lose, forget it for the rest of the event.

FINALLY
Do not feel guilty about having to protest and do not let it affect you for the rest of the race/event. It is as much part of a small boat racing as the odd capsize. However, in neither case do you want it to become a habit.

THE RUN - BY IAN PORTER

For the less experienced the run is seen as a rest during the course of a race - however it should be as tactical as the beat. The same wind shifts and difference of wind strengths will occur across the course and the best path has to be found through them. It is also just as important to sit in the correct position and set sails and centreboard as efficiently as possible. During the mark rounding leading into the run, the boat is borne away and the spinnaker hoisted. The crew would normally go to the windward deck whilst the helm will go to leeward, either sitting on the side deck, or kneeling/crouching where the thwart meets the side deck. His position allows the helm to look backwards and forwards. Look backwards to ensure that boats are not sailing over your wind and to keep an eye on any wind patches coming at slightly differing angles. Look forwards to ensure that you are sailing the most direct route to the next mark. This normally means the longest gybe first, although tidal conditions can upset this rule.

As the spinnaker hoist is a busy period, it is worth checking now that the centreboard has been raised to the correct position. This is not all the way up as the helm uses the centreboard as a pivot. So, no centreboard means lots of helm alterations and thus lower forward speed. I prefer just less than a quarter. At this point it is worth looking up to ensure that the kite is hoisted as high as possible (if you do not have a mark on the spinnaker halyard) and at the same time observe the top sail batten on the mainsail. Ideally, this batten should be square across the centreline of the hull showing that it is also square to the wind. The boom will be against the shroud, but if the kicker is too slack, it will spill air forward and if too tight, it will not allow the sail to spread against the breeze. Next, check the spinnaker pole set, as the helm ensures that the base is spread out and the pole is well to windward. It is important to ensure that the two clews are square across the boat. Lastly, ensure that you are sitting in the correct position. In light airs, aim to maximise waterline length and minimise wetted surface. This will involve the helm sitting on the lee deck, right up against the fully eased boom and the crew sitting well forward nearly against the windward shroud.

It is also important always to sail the boat flat laterally although it can be a little faster sometimes to have a small angle of heel to windward. The varying combinations of helm and crew weights will result in their correct position differing from boat to boat. In medium airs try to get the boat to surf and plane, so both helm and crew would be around the thwart in the middle of the boat. Conversely, in very strong winds, where control is of the utmost importance, the crew and helm should move further aft until both are sitting on the rear locker in the worst conditions! The Wayfarer is a wide-hulled design - loss of control will result in the boat heeling and the rudder coming out off the water, making control even trickier. Again, in exceptional conditions, it pays to let the spinnaker pole go further forward, perhaps to a broad reach position, so that there is less spinnaker to windward and also less chance of it pulling the boat in to windward. This should be completed with the sheet fairly tight to strap down the spinnaker. In these bad conditions, if the boat starts to roll from side to side, place a little extra centreboard down (maybe to a quarter). This will act as a stabiliser and give you a little more steerage although beware, as too much centreboard can cause you to trip up and capsize. The tactics on the run are similar in principle to the beat, in that you are trying to sail the shortest route in distance between two points. Immediately after you have checked your rig set-up, concentration is given to your course path and comparing this to the mark position. It is rare to have a run where both gybes are sailed for the same time period, so the longer gybe is normally sailed first. Whilst sailing down this path, one attempts to maintain pressure in the sails and the crew has a first-hand opportunity to inform the helm when there is good pressure in the spinnaker and when there is not. If the jib starts to want to cross the centreline and one hears the spinnaker rustling (if the cloth is in reasonably good order), you will find that you are sailing too broad or too square down the wind. If you see the crew easing the pole forward to keep the kite full, then you know you are sailing too much of a reach. Again, checking your heading with the mark position can help to keep you on the best track.

Observation behind you will show you where the next puffs are coming from. Are they square to the transom? A puff on the leeward quarter will cause you to head up maybe further away from the shortest path route, whereas the gust on the windward quarter is very good news, for you will be able to sail deeper than your current heading. Waves can give similar results in that as you travel down the front face of a wave, the hull speed increases and often one can use this period of high apparent wind to sail what would normally be a lee run. The result is that this can help shorten the distance to be sailed and give another net gain. Beware though, for as you go through the wave trough and hit the back face of the wave, the true wind will come back with a lot more force so, if you are still sailing your lee run this could be an early bath! When sailing in these waves, also use the period of high speed (i.e. down the front face) to execute your gybe. The low wind force will mean that the boat will gybe easily. In fact, on some large waves the boom will hang over the cockpit on its own, illustrating the wisdom of this point. Again be careful that after the gybe, when sailing into the back of the next wave, if your crew is at the mast changing the pole over and you, as helm, are too far forward, the boat can corkscrew into the wave. In other words, the helm needs to sit or stand as far aft as reasonably possible to maintain boat attitude. Gybe angles come from experience, although I am always amazed by the change in direction necessary to go from run to run. With experience it is possible to gauge the gybe angle just as it is the tacking angle to windward.

Reaching in yachting today will generally show small place gains and losses. However, the run can give huge gains without the toil of the beat. This is no doubt why many of the new breed of skiffs and dinghies choose windward/leeward courses alone. It is therefore worth re-assessing this leg as the one with the most opportunities and dangers.

RACE TACTICS & STRATEGIES

CREWING - BY SIMON TOWNSEND

The ideal crew would have the following qualities:

1. *Unquestioning obedience*
2. *Does not mind getting wet, cold and bored*
3. *Will not bruise easily*
4. *Will not complain when bruised*
5. *Strong, silent and agile*
6. *Enjoys being blamed for things not his/her fault*
7. *Has a bent towards telepathy*
8. *Impeccable time-keeper and recorder of courses*
9. *20/20 vision - for spotting minute buoys*
10. *Likes winning*
11. *Very good loser*

Well, I think that about covers it from the crew's perspective... which probably explains the increase in single-handers about the country!

Teamwork

The crew and helm should preferably be a team at all times, after all, if you don't get on too well off the water what chance have you when spending 2-6 hours together in a competitive and tense 5'x 4' open plan cockpit? How good a team you make will depend greatly on the attitudes and expectations one has of the other. A crew new to sailing cannot be expected to perform as well as one who has been sailing since birth, and likewise it would be unfair of a helm to get him/herself into a situation where the crew had to work at great speed in order to 'save' the helm gybing a spinnaker at the wing mark to a reach in a Force 5 with 2 or 3 boats inside. Other problems arise when their attitudes differ: perhaps the crew is quite happy to just get round the course (although there are days when even this is quite an achievement), while the helm is hell bent on winning. So, try to remember that when you sail a two-man boat you are part of a very integrated team. I have always considered this to be the most important part of dinghy sailing – we are supposed to enjoy it and if you do not like the other part of the crew what chance do you have?

The Helm – as seen by the Crew

For my part I feel a helm is a very intricate creature. They suffer massive mood swings, one moment telling a joke, the next getting paranoid about boat speed. Once they have convinced themselves the boat is slow you can bet the crew will be top of the list to blame. The rule is, try and coax the helm off the boat speed grumble – thereby avoiding the crew grumble! The other strange thing about the helm is the uncanny knack they have of noting everything that is wrong, but never the bits that are right. This applies not only to the crew's efforts but also to any wind shifts, etc. If any boat is moving faster or pointing higher they can see it and always comment, but when they are the 'jammy ones', they never mention it but simply take it for granted that it was about their turn. Better the devil you know. Having said all this, when you do find a helm you are happy with, whether you are racing to win or to improve your sailing, then stick with him/her because as you get to know each other's habits so the enjoyment increases.

The Pre-Race

The pre-race problem I suffer from is getting to the right sailing club at the right time and finding Michael and the boat! Assuming I have accomplished this, there are certain operations I like to complete before the race.

1. *Read the instructions*

Not being a great reader I tend to pick out certain key points, such as signing off/on, starting and finishing procedure (fixed line, gate start etc.), general recall and shortened course and the course itself and whether or not the tea is included.

2. *The Weather Forecast*

Although there is not much you can do about it now.

3. *Clothing*

Based on the weather forecast and experience. There is nothing worse than being too cold and I always like to have the fronts of my legs and shins covered whatever the weather.

4. *Victuals*

Whatever you decide to take in the way of food, always remember to take sufficient water.

5. *The boat*

Always check the boat, not only for poorly tied knots, worn or missing shackles etc., but also check the sheets are running free and led correctly. This can always be done on the water if time is short. There are few worse things than having to re-thread the spinnaker while on the first reach, especially for the helm, as he has to watch the others going past. Mind you, one thing that is worse is sinking on the first reach because you forgot to check the bungs were in!

The Start

Start lines are a wild old place where all sorts of things go on. In reality it's the only time in the race when everyone is together. Although we both have watches it falls to me to count down, usually at minute intervals, until the last one, when I use whatever division I feel is necessary. If you are a long way off the line use shorter divisions to instil a feeling of panic, likewise extend the divisions if you feel you are too close. Two watches are always handy, as it has been known for the buttons to get pressed accidentally or to lose the whole watch prior to the start. Although the helm counting for himself is not ideal, it's better than counting 'elephants' for five minutes! Finally I try to remain in the middle of the boat and try to read the helm's mind as to what manoeuvre is coming next. It often helps if the crew knows what the helm is planning, preferably by the helm telling the crew rather than relying on telepathy. Leaning the boat to leeward moments before the gun then righting it and pulling the sail in gently will aid the boat's acceleration over the line, although my belief is that in anything over a Force 4 the major factor is how far and how long you can lean out, not only on your own, but supporting the helm.

Leaning out Position

Moving on to sitting out, I firmly believe that if it doesn't hurt, you're not doing it right! Some crews will 'hang-on', as is normal in the Star Class. Although this does at first seem easier, it gets harder once the knee joint has been pulled apart – the reason your leg muscles ache less is because you are hanging on your knee ligaments. I believe the correct way is to have the knee joint over the centre of the side decks facing upwards or forwards. If you do it right it hurts like hell and gives you neat bruises on the back of the calf and hamstrings. In light air conditions the crew's job is being perched in the most awkward and uncomfortable position possible whilst still being expected to work the jib.

Beating and Tacking

Once the boat is under way, the crew is most used for watching out for anything the helm may have missed. This ranges from seals in the water to wind shifts or other boats - along with the general crew duties such as keeping the boat flat (whatever the wind strength!) and on occasion altering the jib tension. When tacking I feel it is the helm who leads and the crew who follows – this is particularly true for roll tacks where the team must move together to keep the movement and flow in the boat. To this end I find it easier to watch the helm with one eye and move at the same time and pace as he does, but take into consideration the wind strength i.e. in light conditions it is necessary to move to windward before the tack, but not so afterwards as this would cause the top of the mast to go through 90 degrees more than once. The first beat is without doubt the most important, and the sooner you reach the first mark the easier the rest of the race will become. For this reason it is worth putting all your effort into it — it being easier to hold a good position than fight from behind. Similarly the final beat is also a worthwhile time to work particularly hard as this is generally when others have resigned themselves to their position and are not expecting to be passed.

WINNING THE START – QUENTIN STRAUSS
W7588 Scavenger & W10618 Gorgeous Worgeous

These are my thoughts on starting based on my own experiences, having sailed with a number of top sailors from around the world, in a number of different boats, and at a number of different venues.

Before you go afloat

Read the Starting Section of the Sailing Instructions. Pay particular attention to: the start sequence; the description of the actual starting line (including which exact part of any committee boats); any exclusion zones (including when and when not they apply); and any other exceptions to the Racing Rules of Sailing Rule 26 – Starting Races. Note the time of high/low tide if you are sailing in a tidal area; the relative strength; and any local effects that will become manifest in the start area. Who is your competition? Should you be attacking, defending or just ignoring?

On route to the start

How much is the wind shifting? Are there any timing or direction patterns to the shifts? Are there any permanent wind bends or strength patterns? In a tidal area is one side, or indeed the middle, favoured more than the other? Are the waves flatter one side versus the other? Are there moored boats and/or shipping channels…? This is all about deciding whether or not you have a preference for a side on the first beat, and how strong that preference is. If you have a preference for one side of the beat, generally you should choose the same end of the start line.

At the countdown

As the start approaches, decide between the two of you so it is clear who will be: (a) doing the timing; (b) clocking the race control flags; (c) measuring the distance from the line; (d) looking out for other boats; and, (e) checking the wind direction. Repeat the above, discussing between helm and crew until you are confident of the parameters. Together with the information you have assimilated on route to the start, you should now be able to determine your starting strategy. i.e. which end of the line do you prefer (or indeed the middle) and do you initially want to go left or right. Get a good compass line bearing, sailing up and down the start line, allow for leeward drift and current effects. Sail beyond one or both ends of the line to determine accurate transits. Identify a transit exactly on the line. Go on to identify a conservative transit ALLOWING for the transit to narrow as you approach the other end of the line. At regular intervals go head to wind to identify the wind direction. Prioritise line bias to determine which side of the beat you prefer.

Quentin Strauss (centre) and Stu Rix (helming) write the next two articles - here seen in Melges' leaning out positions

Get an accurate check on the countdown using the warning signal and/or prep. signal as necessary. If necessary resort to the one-minute signal or even ask one of your buddies. Look out for late changes to the start line. These can be obvious when a buoy is lifted and redropped, but easy to miss when the committee boat lengthens or reduces their anchor line.

Thoughts on the best approach to the line
- Use your transit(s) to assess your distance from the line continually. Talk repeatedly about how many boat lengths away you are at its nearest point.

- If you start at either end there is a greater chance of being shut out, but also a greater chance of a start in clear breeze with no boats in your face.

- The ends are generally better if you have better upwind speed than pointing ability. Conversely, the middle is generally good if you have better upwind pointing ability than speed.

- If you start in the middle, your start will be poor unless you have a good transit. There's a greater chance of being impacted by other boats, but also more flexibility with easier options between going left or right up the beat.

- If you arrive relatively early you will have to slow down: (a) that makes it easy for people to slide in next to you; (b) it means your acceleration is the biggest possible hill to climb; (c) it means you have booked your slot and if you can keep your place you will be in the front row.

- Pushing the boom out can make you slow down, even go backwards. Having stopped, lean the boat well over to leeward ahead of the start; sheet in and bring it upright as the gun goes.

- At all costs try to avoid stopping (losing steerage way) or going head to wind.

- If you arrive relatively late you will come in with plenty of speed. That's good in terms of reducing the acceleration mountain to climb, but dangerous in terms of needing a gap where none may exist.

- If you are lined-up on starboard and see someone approaching on port, bear away and point your bow at their bow. This will make it very difficult for them to tack under you. Head up as soon as you can.

- If you are lined-up on starboard and see someone approaching on starboard from behind with more speed, bear away to force him or her either up above you, or so far below, they will not be an issue. Head up as soon as you can.

- Oversheeting the main versus the jib keeps your bow up to the wind.

- Oversheeting the jib versus the main forces your bow away from the wind.

- It is perfect to arrive with a fraction more speed than those around you, wiggle (or tack) the boat to open up the gap you need. The target is to be lined-up behind the part of the line you are targeting, with sufficient time and space to accelerate, boats packed to weather of you with a smallish gap to leeward.

If it all goes wrong
You will know…. for example, you are being squeezed hard or worse you are stuck behind one or several transoms; you have been rolled; you are in irons; you have had to gybe around; there has been a collision. Initially you must try to hang in there and take stock. The best helms will maintain their poor 'lane' rather longer than the less experienced, while the start of the race unfolds and options can be evaluated. It will generally be an option to tack or gybe out, duck transoms and work your way into clear breeze to the right. Often this will make a poor situation worse. One alternative is to point up, but continue going left. Another option is to bear away under the boats in front of you and keep going left. Figure out what is least damaging first, implement second.

Other thoughts and some experiences
- One top tactician, NY, always prioritises favourable line bias ahead of the choice of which side of the beat. Another, TP, does exactly the opposite. Finally another, CP, considers both; his approach is my favourite.

- Phil Stacey and I sailed the 1992 Wayfarer Worlds at Hayling Island, UK in W6777 Wilhelmina. In one race we got shut out at the pin, the line was quite pin biased. We gybed around and started ducking transoms. By the time we finished we were back down at the committee boat with pretty much all 70 odd boats ahead of us heading left. Spirits were low. We went hard right 'banging the corner' pretty much on our own. To be fair we were at the top end of the weight range and the breeze-up conditions suited us. We were flying along and maintaining good height. We turned the windward mark in 2nd place.

- Wendy Howland and I sailed the 2001 Wayfarer Nationals at Medway Yacht Club, UK in W8688 Really Random. In the first race the start area was to one side of the river with the line committee boat biased. The committee boat was to the side of the river, the pin toward the middle of the river and the favourable current. We started pretty much at the pin, sacrificing the line bias but able to get out into the stronger current sooner than most of the 55 other competitors. We led the race from start to finish.

- Stuart Rix, Mike Claxton, Nigel Young and I sailed the 2005 Melges 24 Europeans in Torquay, UK in GBR431 GILL. This team would often start at the pin, indeed, we were noted for it. All week the pin end of the line had a big booby trap. The pin was a flag at the very back of a large committee boat that would lie head to wind. It created a death trap if you got too close. In the countdown to the last race, we noticed the committee boat had suddenly become tide-affected and had swung across the breeze, somewhat on starboard tack. We made a flying pin end start sliding by the committee boat, turned the windward mark in 1st place, came 2nd in the race and in the 75 boat regatta.

- Terry Palmer and I sailed the 2006 Wayfarer Inland Championship at Grafham Water, UK in W7588 Scavenger. In the last race in the countdown, we identified the pin was approaching 10° up over the committee boat end. Our strategy was a pin end start, approaching from the middle of the line. We got an accurate check on the start sequence then reached up and down behind the far end of the line until the final minute. At the final minute we sailed from the pin toward the middle of the line on port tack. It was important to sail toward the bottom of the approaching starboard pack, but not so low that after tacking we would not be able to make it back to the pin.

As the starboard boats approached, first priority was to avoid any rule infringements. Second priority was to assess (a) for individual boats, the time versus distance to the pin; (b) for the pack, the general density. Boats that were early could be let past; we needed to be ahead of boats that were late. Boats that were exactly 'there' time versus distance-wise, we would have to fight with. We picked our spot to tack and were able to win the pin (i.e. the boat that sailed closest to the pin at full speed on starboard tack). We quickly recognised the wind had shifted right in the short period to the start; the line had been square and there would be no options to tack right short of ducking the fleet of some 30 boats. We continued on starboard waiting for the wind to shift back to the left. As we approached the port lay line we started to get anxious, in fact very anxious. Now on the lay line and miracle! The wind shifted back to the left and we tacked. We were comfortably ahead at the windward mark and increased our lead throughout the remainder of the race.

Racing Rules

The current racing rules are the International Sailing Federation (ISAF) Racing Rules of Sailing (RRS) 2009-2012. For guidance as to racing with the Rules, the book '2009-2012 The Rules in Practice', by Bryan Willis (from the 'Sail to Win' Series) is recommended. If you are a newcomer to racing, it is strongly recommended that you keep a keen lookout for other boats, particularly when beating to windward on port, and always steer to avoid a collision anywhere around the course. Discuss the racing rules with regard to any particular situation with a knowledgeable person at the end of the race. That way you will build up experience more safely.

Approaching the start - Race 2 at the International Championships Denmark 2007

WINNING TIPS - BY STUART RIX
National Champion 1994, World Champion 1995
W9363 Mad Savannah

It was drummed into me that the crew who made the least mistakes inevitably won. Sailing is such a complicated sport of many variables: not only is the boat, the rig, the sails and all the tuning involved, but the water, the waves, the tide, and, as if that is not complicated enough, you also have you, the sailor, with all your anxieties and superstitions, your level of commitment and awareness. If you can get all in tune together then the chances are, due to a confident and calm approach, it is you who will make the fewest mistakes, and win!

Tuning

The Wayfarer is an easy boat to sail, but a difficult boat to sail well and fast. There is plenty of good tuning data available from both boatbuilder and sailmaker alike. Certainly the Plus S Series 2 GRP boats are competitive with the wooden boats. This reinforces the One Design principle of the Class, which I believe is important for the development of dinghy racing. I spent invaluable time with both boatbuilder and sailmaker to get what I wanted, and was confident that at the beginning of '94 my boat was going as fast as it had ever been. The Lowestoft Nationals introduced a short chop sea state, especially with the wind in the opposite direction to the tide. For those of us brought up with sailing on inland ponds, this can take a while to adjust to. When sailing on inland water we set up our boats with flatter sails and tight leeches to point higher, but when there is a chop at sea to contend with it is more important to concentrate on boat speed through the waves than pointing ability. To this end I set up my rig to be slightly more upright and with the mast straighter to keep the boat powered up — with the boom on the centreline, no kicker in a light/medium breeze, and the mainsail leech set with a little twist controlled by mainsheet tension. Ease the sheet (inducing twist) when the wind drops or the boat slows down, then, when the boat picks up again or the wind strengthens, tighten the leech again to improve pointing ability. The mainsail leech is an important tool for achieving boat speed, and likewise the genoa is played in the same vein. However, once both crew are sat fully out then I start to let the boom off the centreline and progressively use a lot of kicker to keep the mainsail leech from twisting too much. In a Force 5/6 the boom is well off the quarter of the transom and being played around this position to keep the boat as flat as possible in any gusts, with the kicking strap on as hard as I can pull it (12:1 system). The genoa car is moved back 2" and the sheet eased 1".

Tactics

So, having got your boat set up well for all conditions, it is now time to forget about fiddling for boat speed (if only we could!) and concentrate on sailing the best course. It is no good having the fastest boat if you point it in the wrong direction — you only end up in the wrong place quicker!

Let's start at the beginning. If you start well you have already accomplished 30/40% of the race tactics – certainly in a big fleet. If you do not get away in the first echelon of boats then you are immediately in dirty wind and going slower. It is very important to be sailing at full speed on the line when the gun goes, ideally with no one on top of you or beneath you, squeezing you up. It's not easy. It was Gary Player who said 'the more I practise the luckier I get.' Every now and again you should be over the line, showing how close you are pushing it. But which end of the line should I start?

Where is the line bias? On a long line you cannot afford to give everyone the luxury of a head start by starting at the wrong end.

Tide/wind bends? Do I want to go left or right, depending on what is going to happen further up the course, and will that modify 1 above?

You need to collect all the information available to you and produce a plan of where to start and which way to go, and more importantly, stick to it ...

When it all works ...

On Race 4 at the Nationals I decided I wanted to go hard left towards the shore to try to get out of the tide, which was over the course. So, I started down at the port end to start going in that direction immediately, got away well and led the bunch of boats that went left. I had a tactical plan, executed it well, was not distracted from it, and eventually won the race.

When it all goes wrong ...

But what if it all does not go well. In Race 2 after a good start I went hard left and made the Big Mistake (huge!) of overstanding the windward mark by a long way. I rounded the windward mark 12th/13th with the leaders long gone. Now, what I must do, as I am unlikely to win the race, is adopt a policy of minimum damage. Consistency wins Championships. I therefore sailed the fastest straight line speed (allowing for tide) down the next two reaches, concentrating on surfing on the waves (Force 4/5), not getting involved with any luffing matches and trying to calm the mind (busy castigating me for being such a plonker up the first beat!). The latter was the hardest to achieve. It took me a complete round before I forgave myself the mistake and got on with the task in hand. Not till then did we start to go quickly again – finally finishing fifth, which proved to be an important discard. Mistakes will happen. You and I must put them behind us quickly. Having tuned the boat, decided the tactics, then it is down to between the ears to win the race.

Mind over matter

Several years ago a survey placed sailing and motor sport at the top level of sports demanding a developed intellect. The complexity of these two activities, the sophisticated equipment involved and the variability of the conditions that they have to operate, make the qualities of knowledge, analysis and logic essential to success. Mix this with the anxiousness of a big race ... and the self-doubting 'jelly' at the back of the boat is in trouble!

All sailors get psyched out at times. It is so easy to say 'the other helm is going faster,' or 'the other helm is pointing higher.' In reality this is rarely the case. However, if you keep thinking it the other helm soon will be! It stands to reason, if you are concentrating on the opposition's boat and not focused on your own, you will begin to slow down. There will be times when the other helm gets a lift or gust of wind that you do not, that's the way it goes. You must continue to focus and be aware of your boat, the boats around you, the orientation of the course, the wind, the waves and what the tide is doing. Easy isn't it? All it is, is practice and learning from mistakes.

The deciding race of the Championships

Going into the final race of the Nationals, I stood quarter of a point behind 'a legend in his own lifetime.' I had to beat him over the water and finish in the top 5 to win the Championship. I knew my boat was as fast as anyone's in the breeze of the day and, importantly, so did everyone else. After a number of attempts the race was started and we got away to a good start leading the bunch of boats to the left-hand side of the course as planned. Now to get to the windward mark first and away... not to be! The boats from the right-hand side got there first. We go round 5th and McNamara 7th. My crew reminds me to 'settle down and think of boat speed,' which he had been invaluable at doing all week. Despite making a mistake up the second beat, allowing Michael to cross us, we quickly picked the best course. We knew the boat was fast, so were able to relax and enjoy the sail, the result being that we were second going round the last leeward mark and Michael McNamara was third. Priority one was to stay ahead of him but also to remain in the top of the fleet. We covered hard initially and then eased off to maintain general position and then, in the last quarter of the final beat covered hard again once second or third position overall seemed assured. Hence I achieved a goal set a number of years earlier – to win the Wayfarer Championships – through practice and learning from mistakes. We formed a well-tuned boat and crew who, given their day and a little bit of luck, would take the championship from a field of very good sailors. Yes!

WAYS TO LOSE A SAILBOAT RACE
by Earl Schnur

The Start

Do not find which end of the line is favoured. **Give the other boats a two or three boat length lead at the start!** To find the favoured end, sail on a reach to the pin end of the line and head straight to windward outside the pin. While sitting head to wind, sight across the pin toward the committee boat. If the committee boat is forward of abeam, that end is favoured.

Do not hoist the spinnaker before the start to make sure it is rigged properly. **You were embarrassed to beat everyone to the first mark anyway and you want him or her to drive over you on the first reach so that you can try to play catch up.** Run the spinnaker up and down at least once, then store it on the port side so that you can fly it on the first reach of a buoys to port course with no twisted lines, missing pole, etc.

Do not time the line. You may be forced on to the line early and have to reach down the line. If you do not have enough time to reach down the line, you will have to gybe around and go off on port below the whole fleet. *Instant last!* Sail from the committee boat to the pin, noting the time required. This will usually not change during the starting sequence.

Wander away from the line in light air. It may take you two or three minutes to get to the line if there is no breeze. **By now the rest of the boats are gone.** In light weather, never be more than fifty feet or so from the line, preferably close to the favoured end. Be luffing in the right area with about one minute to go; no one can move you if you are not moving very fast and on starboard tack near head to wind.

Do not know how long it takes to get from where you are to the line. **Guarantee that you will be early or late.** Get a feel for how fast your boat accelerates from a luffing condition and know how long it will take to get to the line from where you are luffing. You can practise this at the committee boat early in the pre-start manoeuvres. Many good sailors hold such a position and accelerate to the line with just five seconds left.

Start at the port end of the line on starboard tack. **If the fleet is headed after the start, you are ahead but sailing in the wrong direction and will get to tack last.** If the fleet is lifted, the rest of the fleet is ahead of you. Find a way to start somewhere in the right hand 25% of the fleet. This will allow you some freedom to move up the centre of the course.

Be going slowly as you can across the line. **Give everyone else a nice feeling while they grind over you as they cross the line.** Instant second row start. Eat bad air for half the first leg. Make sure your boat is moving at or near top speed as you come across the line. Luff up before the start to get some room below you so that you can reach off a bit to get some speed up. Go for speed over pointing at the start. Once it is safe to do so, you can shift into pointing mode.

The First beat

Stay on starboard and go left. **Guarantee that every boat you meet after you tack will have the right of way.** Three or four ducked transoms and you are now three or four boat lengths behind the leaders. Tack to port when the wind is right and the opportunity presents itself. Favour the right side of the course. When you meet boats as you come back into the middle, you can force them left or tack on top of them. Either way, the odds are in your favour.

Take the short tack first. **That way, any lift that obviates the necessity for that short tack will have you reaching and going faster than the rest of the fleet. Of course, they will have much less distance to sail, but so what?** Take the long tack first (the tack that is significantly less than 45 degrees to the mark). This guarantees you a benefit from any shift over the boats already on the lay line.

Sail right to the lay line. **Make sure that any boat inside of you gets the advantage from any wind shift.** If you are on the lay line early, a lift has you reaching for the mark and you will be sailing a longer distance than the rest of the boats. A header allows the inside boats to tack and still sail a shorter course than you. Stay near the rhumb line and do not go out to the lay line until late in the beat. This gives you freedom to play the shifts and sail the shortest course.

Underlay the windward mark. **Be forced to take one more tack on to port with a host of starboard boats coming up.** Get a chance to lose four or five boats because of greed. Give yourself some leeway at the mark. Hitting the mark is a fine way to spoil your day.

The First Reach

Do not look around. Just set the spinnaker immediately. **Let the rest of the boats go up to windward and blanket you.** While they roar off towards the gybe mark, you lose some more because now it turns out that the reach was too tight for a spinnaker. Reach up to windward a bit and get a fix on the next mark. Allow no one to go to windward of you. Set the spinnaker in slow motion so that it actually happens fast. Go down with the puffs to stay in them longer, and up in the light spots to reach the next puff quicker.

Make sure you are the outside boat going around the gybe mark. **That way you can watch all the inside boats gybe before you.** Note how well they make their boats go in clear air while your tell-tales revolve like beanie spinners in their wind shadow. Get inside on the first mark, even if you have to slow down. This way you will start the second reach with clear air that will keep you in the race and in control of your strategy.

Make sure you mess up the spinnaker gybe. **The trailing boats appreciate the boat lengths this costs you.** Work hard at perfecting your spinnaker gybes. At the very least, make sure the spinnaker ends up on the new leeward side of the boat after the gybe and get the main and jib drawing immediately after the gybe. As at the start of the reach, do not let them pass you to windward. If necessary, let the spinnaker hang to leeward with the guy pre-cleated while you and your crew fight off those who would steal your wind. Once this is settled, get the pole on and spinnaker away!

The Leeward Mark
Do not clear the halyard or take the spinnaker down a bit early. A little excitement with a fouled spinnaker at the mark is just what you need to make the pizza taste better on the way home! Clear the halyard and get the spinnaker into the boat a bit early so that you can concentrate on tactics at the rounding.

Make sure you round wide so that the hot shot following you has room to round up inside you and sail a little higher and a little faster. You enjoy lying awake for a few hours with a knot in your stomach, wondering why you did not think ahead a bit. Avoid tacking for a while after rounding the mark even if you have to eat some bad air. Wait until you get up to speed and until your tack will put you into clear air.

Second Beat
Forget about the rest of the fleet. You know where the wind will be. And you do not like to mix it up anyway. It is always fun to watch the boats that were behind you ride up a lift on the other side of the course while you hobby horse in the power boat swells. Keep a loose cover on your competition. A win by four seconds counts just as much as one by four minutes. They cannot pass you if you stay between them and the windward mark – unless they are better sailors in which case they will pass you anyway!

The Run
Break out a can of soda, sit on the transom and enjoy life. No race is ever won on a run anyway. Watch the sharp boats ride down the streaks and pass you on both sides! Pay attention to the wind streaks on the water. You will go much faster if you can find and stay in one. If it lightens up, look for another streak and reach over to it. Then run down with it. Sail smart on the runs and soon everyone will be telling you how fast your boat is downwind.

The Final Beat
Do not cover anyone since you are way ahead. You have the race won since no one has been able to match your upwind speed all day. Think a lot about that fact as they are handing out the hardware to the two boats that caught you. It is even more important to cover on the last beat because you can make the following boats do desperate things since there is no tomorrow.

Do not figure out which end of the finish line is favoured. Who cares? As you zip along the finish line on starboard, you make three port tackers bear off to go behind you. Compared to a thrill such as that, what does it matter if they all finished before you did because you were sailing along the line while they crossed it? Decide which end of the line is favoured early enough to go there by the shortest possible route. Nothing else matters (as long as you do not foul anyone in the process).

SPINNAKER HANDLING - THE ALTERNATIVE APPROACH
Cath Longhurst & Tracey Newman

Hoisting
Arrive with little time to spare before the race; rig quickly, go afloat. On approaching the windward mark, the helm and crew start a debate about wind strength and discuss the merits of swimming. Having reached the 'helm's consensus', the helm begins the spinnaker hoist; the spinnaker reaches the top of the jib and gets stuck between the jib halyard and forestay; the crew is dispatched onto the foredeck to sort out the problem and gets overtaken by the slowest boats in the fleet. The helm drops the spinnaker, the crew re-rigs the spinnaker halyard and the helm re-hoists the spinnaker just in time for the gybe mark!

The Gybe Mark
Both helm and crew fail to notice that no one else is flying their kite as the next reach is too tight; the helm calls the gybe; the crew disagrees but is encouraged to complete the manoeuvre anyway. The crew helps to gybe the main; but the spinnaker is now flying inside out between the jib and the main. The helm realises the reach is too tight and calls for the spinnaker drop.

Dropping
The helm releases the spinnaker halyard and drops the spinnaker; the crew scrabbles to pull it into the chute but can't. The spinnaker falls over the side and becomes a sea anchor; the sheet runs right under boat and catches on the centreboard. The helm and crew exchange pleasantries while both pulling as hard as possible on the spinnaker sheet helping to slow the boat even more. The crew eventually unties the spinnaker at the clews and recovers the spinnaker into the cockpit. The helm sails back to the clubhouse to write a crew wanted ad!

CRUISING GUIDE & STRATEGIES

Introduction
This chapter covers all aspects of non-racing sailing activity, from a gentle family sail, to ambitious open sea voyages. While the most obvious difference from racing is that cruising is not competitive, it should also be noted that whilst racers can usually rely on the support of safety boats, cruisers generally need to be much more self-reliant. Over the last fifty years, Wayfarers have cruised in most locations normally visited by larger yachts, with the Wayfarer having the advantage of being able to explore much shallower bays, beaches and backwaters; places yachts wouldn't normally dare venture. The ease of trailing by road and ferry also opens up further cruising options compared to a yacht. A Wayfarer may not always be able to compete with a yacht's comfort factor - but it can offer a far greater cruising experience, at a fraction of the cost.

Cruising Areas
Cruising areas may be divided into protected, (inland); semi-protected, (estuary, coastal sea); and unprotected, (open sea). This division can often depend as much on the weather conditions, as the location. It is strongly advised that people broaden their experience and sailing skills in stronger winds in known and safe sailing areas, before venturing out into more demanding and unfamiliar territory. By gradually acquiring experience over a number of years, it is possible to develop the skills needed to sail in more demanding areas, like the wilder parts of the Scottish west or north coasts. The hazards of this type of coastline can include the often-inclement weather; the rocky nature of the coast; the fast-flowing tidal streams between the islands; and the long distances between beaches or havens offering a safe place of refuge. By way of compensation, the coastal scenery is incomparable – beautiful, wild, remote, sparsely populated, unpolluted, and unspoilt.

Gaining Experience
The UKWA organises various cruising rallies each year, as well as two specific training events. The Spring Cruising Conference is an ideal 'starting out' opportunity for anyone new to cruising and day sailing, as well as being helpful to those with some experience, and who wish to add to their knowledge and techniques of Wayfarer cruising. The event combines talks and demonstrations on all aspects of cruising with examples of how the more experienced cruisers rig and equip their boats. The Tidal Training course is a more practical sailing skills training event, which offers both theory and practice sessions on sailing in tidal waters. An excellent way to sharpen boat-handling skills for day sailing and cruising is to join a local sailing club and take part in racing events! Since racing always has rescue cover available, it offers an ideal opportunity to experience sailing in conditions and wind strengths that would be considered too demanding and potentially dangerous for an unsupported cruise or day sail.

Sailing Solo
The Wayfarer can be sailed solo without any difficulty – with the most demanding part usually being the solo launching and retrieval of the boat. It is wise to fit up to two sets of slab reefing points on the mainsail and a good genoa furling or reefing system, so that the process of reducing sail can be carried out quickly and easily. This is all explained in the 'Comfort and Safety Zone' Chapter. All controls need to be led back to the helm, and the jib sheeting arrangement made easy for the helm to work and cleat. Sailing close to the wind, and hence going about, can be more difficult in stronger wind conditions, but can easily be mastered. Whenever the wind does become too strong for solo sailing, it should always be possible to run under jib only to a safe haven. Some solo Wayfarer owners have fitted steel centreboards to their boats. This does provide for a similar weight advantage as having a crew when sailing close hauled, and greatly reduces the chances of capsizing. This modification however does put the Wayfarer out of class, and is not recommended, since unless the area is suitably strengthened, the fitting can weaken the centre case housing, thereby compromising the structure of the hull.

Launch Site Directory
A useful source of information for cruisers planning to sail in an unfamiliar area is the Launch Site Directory on the UKWA website - www.wayfarer.org.uk

Rallies
An alternative way of finding out useful information in an unfamiliar sailing area is to join a UKWA organised Wayfarer Rally, where the launching, and all suitable stopping points are organised by a person with local knowledge. The UKWA organises rallies and cruises in many different parts of the UK. These are designed to introduce members to any new area they might wish to sail, and to provide an opportunity to progress to another level of sailing experience. There are usually a number of experienced cruisers on each rally, who are always willing to share their knowledge and experience. The Wayfarer International Committee (WIC) also runs an International rally each year, with members attending from the UK, Scandinavian, Dutch, Canadian, and US Wayfarer Associations. These are becoming an increasingly popular way of sailing in a completely new environment. Countries visited so far have been Norway, Sweden, Denmark, Holland, France, Ireland, Canada, and the U.S.A. Further information on these, and other overseas events, can be found on the Events page of www.wayfarer.org.uk. Details of all events are published in 'Wayfarer News' too.

UKWA Rally Sailing Experience Guide

In order to ensure members are aware of the level of experience required for any particular rally, each is given a grading. This guide should enable you to choose a rally at your present level of experience, and gradually work your way to a more advanced level. This experience guide is also relevant for anyone setting sail individually in the cruising areas listed.

Inland Sailing — Helm should be able to manoeuvre boat in a moderate breeze (up to force 4) without risk of colliding with accompanying Wayfarers.

Estuary Sailing — Helm should be able to manoeuvre the boat in a fresh breeze (up to Force 5), and be competent at reefing afloat, man overboard, anchoring, and capsize recovery.

Sea Sailing — Both helm and crew should be experienced in handling their boat in a strong breeze and moderate to rough sea conditions (Force 5+) and be competent and experienced in reefing afloat, anchoring, and capsize recovery (including inversion). They should also be aware of tides, and able to use their own chart of the area for a passage plan.

Advanced Open Sea — For those with considerable sea sailing experience and fully competent at navigation to make a detailed passage plan for the cruise.

Gentlemen at lunch at a Brancaster Cruising Rally

Guidelines for Tidal Day Sailing and Cruising

This set of guidelines is primarily intended for anyone embarking on anything more ambitious than a simple sail in a well-protected area with quick and easy access to the launch/retrieval site, although most of the points are valid for any type of sailing being undertaken.

Are you familiar with the area you propose to sail?
Have as much knowledge as possible about the area you are sailing. If you have not sailed in that particular area before, it is advisable to seek local knowledge before setting out.

CRUISING GUIDE & STRATEGIES

Is the boat in sound and good working order?

Make sure the boat is sound and everything is in good working order. Both the boat and its equipment can be quite old, yet still be in perfect order to sail; but the older the boat is, the more carefully the gear needs to be checked over. It is generally cheaper and more cost effective to replace items before they finally break! Make sure that both the centreboard and rudder (and particularly the fittings securing these to the boat) are completely sound. Check that the front and rear buoyancy hatches are properly secured and the seal will be watertight in the event of a capsize. It will not be possible to sail the boat again if either of the buoyancy tanks are full of water after capsizing, and it will be necessary for a rescue boat to tow the capsized, probably inverted, boat ashore – breaking the mast in the process. Check both the standing rigging (supporting the mast), and running rigging (securing the sails), to make sure that all is sound, and nothing is likely to fail whilst out sailing.

Arrival at Ipswich Lock - International Rally in Suffolk 2005

Are you properly equipped?

For any estuary or sea sailing, it is always advisable to take an anchor, chain and line. A small grapnel anchor is not generally good enough to hold the boat in the conditions when anchoring is most likely to be needed - in a strong wind and/or tide. Most experienced cruisers take at least a 2.5kg Danforth or CQR with a minimum of one metre of chain (weighing approximately one kilogram) and at least thirty metres of anchor line.

It is advisable to take a pair of oars on any cruise, so that if difficulties are encountered, it is possible to row to safety. A paddle - preferably with a long shaft - is useful to manoeuvre the boat, or to add a little extra speed over a short distance. It is essential to have at least one set of reefing points in the mainsail, so that the sail area can be readily reduced to suit the prevailing conditions, thereby making the sailing far more comfortable in stronger wind conditions. See next chapter 'Comfort & Safety Zone' for details

It is important that all crew are wearing personal buoyancy, and adequately clothed for the duration of the sail. Additional warm and windproof clothing should always be available in the front or rear locker (preferably in a waterproof bag) in case the need arises. A nutritious snack and something to drink should also be included in the list of essential supplies, in case a trip is of a longer duration than expected.

When setting out, it is advisable to start any trip up wind, or up tide whenever possible, so that the return trip is relatively quick, and a much easier sail.

Setting out for Cundy's Island - International Rally Maine USA 2008

Keep a good look out for other boats of all sizes. The best rule of the road for day sailing and cruising is to keep out of everyone else's way! Always aim to go well behind other boats, rather than cross in front. A collision is more likely to be averted in any emergency situation by steering to windward to go about or slow down, rather than by bearing away. Remember Rule 8 of the IRPC (International Rules for Prevention of Collisions at Sea) 'any alteration of course/speed to avoid collision shall... be large enough to be readily apparent to another vessel...'

Guidelines for extended Tidal Cruising

Whilst the following points are essential for any extended sea cruising, probably the most important aspect is for both the helm and crew to have sufficient sailing skills and experience to undertake the trip, particularly in any worsening weather situation.

Boat equipment
Check all fittings thoroughly and equip the boat adequately for the needs of any particular trip. Consider fitting an airbag in a sail head buoyancy pocket to minimise the risk of the boat inverting should the boat capsize. It is always advisable to make sure everything is tied into the boat in case of a capsize, or any other eventuality.

GPS, Maps, Charts and knowledge of the area
Obtain detailed maps or charts of the area you plan to sail, and list any safe havens to run to in the event of the weather conditions worsening. It is well worth investing in one of the latest types of GPS, which show an on-screen position relative to a detailed chart of the coastline - subject to also purchasing the relevant chart card. Bear in mind that these instruments can fail at any time however, and information should always be backed up on a waterproofed paper chart.

Tide tables
A set of tide tables is always necessary for cruising in tidal waters in order to use the tides to best advantage, or at least to minimise their disadvantage.

Weather forecast
Obtain a good weather forecast. It is always best either to postpone the trip if the weather is unfavourable, or find an alternative destination or area to sail.

Accommodation
When planning an overnight trip, check beforehand that there is a suitable landing place, and the boat or land tent to be used is fully functional, (or check for possible alternative accommodation). This might be more challenging when cruising abroad!

Alternative Power
It is advisable to carry a small outboard, as well as a pair of oars, if it is essential to reach a desired destination by a particular time.

The gear for a serious sea cruise must all be fitted in tidily & securely - the helm & crew knowing the location of everything!

Notify the Coastguard
Notify the Coastguard of any extended trip at sea, with a passage plan giving the planned route and estimated start and arrival times, together with the essential details of the boat (by completing in a CG 66 form – obtainable online from the Coastguard: www.mcga.gov.uk – search – CG66). Phone a contact person ashore immediately before leaving, and give an ETA. If the shore contact is not called within a reasonable time of the expected arrival time, they can then inform the Coastguard that you are overdue at your expected destination. The Coastguard would much prefer to know about any serious cruising trip, together with details of the boat, so that they are aware of the background situation should any problems arise. It is less than helpful for them to be informed of a missing Wayfarer, for which they have no details or information about the cruise that boat was attempting. The local coastguard can be extremely helpful and supportive, offering excellent advice.

Guidelines for Open Sea Sailing
Perhaps the most important safety advice for Open Sea sailing is to have the experience of many years of coastal sea sailing, with the boat equipped for just about any eventuality – because your life can most certainly depend on it. You will be out there, on your own, with very little chance of any assistance should you find yourself in the unfortunate situation of needing support.

Day Skipper, Coastal, Skipper/Yacht Master Offshore
Helms should gain at least RYA Day Skipper, and preferably Coastal Skipper, or Yacht Master Offshore qualifications. Experience should be gained when coastal cruising of using compass and charts to check on navigation, and to back up any information given by a hand-held GPS. Remember that navigation may well have to be done in hostile conditions when out at sea, and all navigation equipment needs to be made weatherproof.

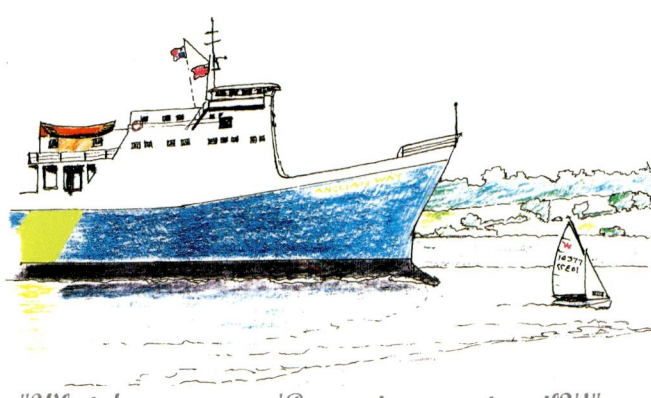

"What do you mean - 'Power gives way to sail?'!"

Outboard Motor
It is essential to carry an outboard when crossing shipping lanes, which should always be planned to be crossed in daylight. Outboards can also be extremely useful and are sometimes essential due to regulations when approaching a busy harbour, or when encountering a strong tidal flow approaching landfall. The facilities provided by a marina or sailing club are usually extremely welcoming after a long sea cruise, and well worth taking into consideration when choosing a point of landfall.

Radar reflector and white masthead light
It is wise to carry a good radar reflector, so that it is possible to be picked up on a ship's radar, as well as a strong all round white mast head light, powerful enough to be seen from a good distance, and with sufficient power back-up for it to be lit for the complete period of darkness.

GPS, VHF, and Flares
Hand held GPS's have become so relatively inexpensive that it would be most unwise not to use one for any serious coastal or open sea trip. Similarly, a waterproof VHF hand-held radio is another essential item for anyone undertaking a sea cruise. Be aware that it is sometimes possible for the Coastguard or someone from another ship to receive a signal, even if you cannot receive them. Flares should also always be carried, though it should be borne in mind if way out at sea, that they might not necessarily work, or even when they do, may not be seen by a passing ship.

Lifelines
Both helm and crew should always wear a lifeline, anchored to a strong point on the boat, whenever a man overboard rescue would not be straightforward. This is particularly relevant at night, in fog, or in strong winds. If someone becomes detached from the boat in adverse conditions without a harness and lifeline, then the chances of survival are minimal.

Cruising Logs
Writing a log of any trip is always worthwhile. It helps record the trip for later posterity, and gives a greater sense of achievement to the experience. It is always helpful to list any mistakes that might have been made; since it makes it less likely that these will be repeated on any later cruise, as well as helping others to learn from the experience – should the log be made available to members through the Log Library.

The UKWA has two cruising trophies, which are awarded annually. The Viking Trophy, a silver plate model of a Viking Longship, was presented to the Association by Frank Dye to commemorate his Wayfarer voyages to Iceland and Norway.

International Rally Friesland Holland 2006 - The luxury of mothership 'In Dubio' greatly extended the cruising range

It is awarded for the best log of a cruise undertaken during the previous year. The cruise does not have to be in any way adventurous, since the award is for the quality of the write-up and related photos, rather than the epic nature of any trip.

The Piers Plowman Trophy was given by Greta Plowman in memory of her husband, Piers, with whom she had many memorable cruises in Britain and abroad. It is a wooden platter engraved with the Plough constellation, and is awarded for the best write up of a Wayfarer event submitted to the magazine editor for publication in 'Wayfarer News'.

Cruising Log Library

The Association has an extensive library of logs of Wayfarer Cruises all around the UK, as well as many parts of Europe and North America. These not only provide interesting reading material on the various aspects of Wayfarer cruising, but are also a useful source of information for anyone wishing to cruise a particular area. Individual cruising logs are available to UKWA members from the Website (www.wayfarer.org.uk – Cruising – Library), or from the Log Librarian (details on Website).

Checklist of Equipment for cruising

Boat
Mainsail with battens and reefing system, preferably reefing genoa and/or jib. Main sheet, genoa sheets
Spinnaker*, spinnaker sheets*, pole* or whisker pole*
Rudder and tiller. Fenders/boat rollers. Anchor, warp and chain, painter and rope for mooring. Oars*, rowlocks*, paddle. Outboard engine*, spare fuel* and spare parts*. Bucket(s).

Living Aboard
Boat tent and supports. Sleeping bag and mattress. Stove, fuel, lighter and/or matches with spare fuel bottles/cartridges Torch and/or cabin lamp with spare batteries. Food and water in suitable containers.   Kettle* and/or nesting saucepans. Knives, forks, spoons, can/bottle opener etc. Bowls/plates, mugs (preferably with lids). First aid kit, sun-cream, insect repellent, survival bag.* Plastic bags (useful for waste items etc.) clothes pegs and line*.

Navigation
Steering compass (mounted on the boat), and hand-bearing compass. Charts, land (OS) maps*, tide tables, pilot book. Pencil(s) – including chinagraph, for writing on plastic covering of charts. Dividers*, Breton plotter*. GPS and VHF and FM/Long/Short wave Radio with spare batteries. Flares and Fog horn*

Note: * = Optional items

Useful Equipment to carry for Spares and Repairs
Stainless steel shackles, clevis pins, split rings, a few assorted sizes of stainless steel screws, duck and/or insulation tape, shockcord ties. Multi-tool knife set, short handled screwdrivers for slotted and pozi-headed screws, hacksaw blade, small hand drill, drill bits, small piece of emery cloth.

Wood and GRP repairs
Sections of thin plywood to make temporary repairs to holes in the hull. These can be secured with stainless steel screws. Once the main hole is plugged, tape can be applied to make it watertight. A piece of thick polythene to tape over any damage to hull that has not created a hole.

Sails and Rigging
Spinnaker repair tape for emergency repair to sails, particularly if it is stitched on after being applied over any tear. A spare shroud wire may be useful, though the redundant forestay can always be used as an emergency shroud. Spare lengths of rope. Some of the above items may be worth carrying in the car for short day trips, but are best carried in the Wayfarer for longer cruising trips.

Stowage
The Wayfarer has excelled itself as a cruising boat, mainly because of its stability and its capacity for carrying cruising gear, particularly in the front and rear buoyancy tanks. It should be remembered however, that these are primarily buoyancy (air) tanks and not storage lockers, and should never be filled so full of gear that there is little air capacity left. Under no circumstances should the polystyrene blocks in the buoyancy tanks be removed in order to create more storage space, as these are fitted to keep the Wayfarer just afloat in the worst-case scenario of the buoyancy tanks filling with water. The Wayfarer World and Mark IV have optional rear stowage tanks separate from the built-in buoyancy.

Watertight plastic storage containers used to good effect on this Wayfarer World

Watertight plastic storage containers with large lids, usually available from marine chandlers, are a useful way of storing gear that needs to be kept dry. Waterproof dri-bags are particularly useful for clothing and sleeping gear. It is worth expelling as much air as possible before sealing these bags, as this can considerably reduce their overall size. It is also advisable to ensure the bags are not pushed into areas with any rough surface of glass fibre, or where there is anything with a sharp point - like a split ring of a clevis pin on the mast pivot bolt, which is likely to damage the integrity of the bag. Each cruiser generally has their own particular preference for the way in which the many items of gear are stowed on their Wayfarer. It is however of the greatest importance that the anchor and chain are stored well away from the compass, whatever the preference is for other items. For those new to Wayfarer cruising, the best way to get ideas on storage is to attend the Winter Cruising Conference or Wayfarer rallies, where nobody will mind you poking about looking over other members' boats - it has almost become a Wayfarer ritual - which helps keep everyone abreast with the latest cruising ideas and developments.

The optional auxiliary rear box of the Mark IV Wayfarer has been designed to hold a 4HP size of outboard.

Pumps and Bailers

Sailing to windward on a long cruise in conditions that cause spray to come over the foredeck usually results in a considerable amount of water being shipped aboard. This additional weight can greatly slow the progress of the boat.

Self-bailers (with the exception of the later 'World' and Mk IV versions) do not generally remedy this, as the weight of gear normally carried by cruisers prevents the boat from gaining sufficient speed. Cruisers therefore tend to resort to pumps to remove excess water from the boat.

The diaphragm type of pump is by far the most efficient. It is best mounted so that it can be operated by the crew, whilst sailing to windward. This is usually around the front seat area, and as far out of the way of the jib sheets as possible. However, the best place yet found for the pump (with a detachable handle) is under the side deck, with the outlet tube being led to the back of the boat. In this position, the pump can be operated by either the helm or the crew, and is completely out of the way when not in use. Ideally, for those doing extensive cruising, a pump should be mounted on each side of the boat, with the inlet pipe running to the opposite side of the boat.

A cheaper lift, or draw type pump can be quite adequate, although it requires more effort to work, and is rather more difficult to operate whilst sailing, since it barely works efficiently enough to enable a long inlet pipe to run to the opposite side of the boat.

Self-bailers are always worth fitting, since they work well when sailing at a reasonable speed, (usually only off the wind when cruising), and will completely empty the boat of water. It is also an easier method of draining water from the bottom of the boat after it has been brought ashore, than opening the drain plugs in the stern and the rear buoyancy tank. Care does need to be taken not to get sand or grit in the self-bailers, however, since they may then leak, which can cause problems when sleeping in the boat on a cruise. Whilst on the subject of removing water from the boat, it is worth carrying at least one bucket for bailing the water out after capsizing. A bucket can also serve another useful purpose – cruisers are not known as the 'bucket and chuck it' brigade for nothing – although for men at least, a washing conditioner bottle can be more convenient.

Rowing

It can be useful to carry a pair of oars for cruising, even when an outboard is normally carried, since a motor is never guaranteed to work, and there is always a limit to the amount of fuel that can be reasonably carried. They should be as long as can be easily stored in the boat - either on the seats and up under the foredeck, or on the floor either side of the centreplate housing. The minimum length for an oar should be around 2.45m, but because of the wide beam of a Wayfarer, this length does not make for comfortable rowing over any great distance. A better length is 2.6m, and more ideally 2.75m. Ultimately the length of oar is determined by the available storage space, and the cost. Weight is also a factor which should be should be taken into consideration when purchasing oars, with some type or makes of oar much heavier than others.

The rowlocks should be fitted about 30mm in from the edge of the gunwale, (which is as close to the edge of the gunwale as is possible), and between 260mm and 300mm (10in to 12in) aft of the back edge of the thwart. This area should have been reinforced when the boat was made, so it is worth looking under the side deck to find the position of the reinforcement. It is advisable to contact the Cruising Secretary for advice if fitting rowlocks to a Wayfarer World, or Mk IV. It is normally necessary to insert a chock under the rowlock to raise the oar, in order to prevent it chafing on the gunwale whilst rowing.

Paddling

A paddle is generally only useful to manoeuvre the boat in a confined area, or to add a little extra speed over a short distance. It is an inefficient means of propulsion over a long distance. A paddle with a long shaft is the most convenient to use – with a Canadian canoe paddle up to 1.6m long being ideal. It is generally easiest to sit on the bow when needing to manoeuvre the boat, which makes it possible to paddle in various directions to move the boat in whichever way is needed. When a little extra speed is required, say to make headway against a particularly strong current, the paddle is best used by the crew over the side of the boat. A paddle is used to its greatest efficiency when the upper hand is placed on the top of the paddle, and a leverage action of pushing with the top hand, and pulling with the lower hand is used. It is not nearly so effective to grip the stem of the paddle with both hands and use only a pulling action.

Outboards

The decision to carry an outboard or not rather depends on your views of cruising. An outboard is obviously not for the sailing purists, for whom a noisy motor would spoil the pleasure of the trip, and who are happy to row if the wind drops, or anchor until the wind picks up again. On the other hand, an outboard can be an extremely useful method of getting out of trouble if being carried into a difficult situation, or to get to a planned destination should the wind die. It can also be used to advantage to motor-sail in very light wind conditions.

Engine Size

A 2 HP to 3.5 HP outboard is quite sufficient to power a Wayfarer, even in tidal waters. A 4 HP outboard is heavier and more expensive than the smaller outboards; though does have the advantage of an external fuel supply which saves leaning over the back of the boat to add fuel to the tank when at sea, as well as a reverse gear - the smaller outboards needing to be rotated 180° for reverse. A standard size shaft is quite sufficient, since a longer shaft means the propeller is lower in the water, and thereby more likely to ground in shallow water – possibly damaging the propeller and/or breaking the shear pin. Greater propeller depth for a short shaft motor can easily be achieved by the helm and crew moving their weight aft.

Outboard Noise and Vibration

Outboards can vary considerably in noise and vibration – both of which can be tolerated for relatively short periods, where, for example, the outboard might be used to manoeuvre the boat into a position to rig the sails, but become less bearable the longer the motor is used. Generally, water-cooled engines are much quieter than air-cooled engines, and those with a heavier flywheel will run more smoothly, causing less vibration. The disadvantage of a water-cooled engine is that the impeller needs to be checked/changed regularly to ensure the cooling system works when the engine is needed, and a heavier flywheel increases the overall weight of the motor. Day sailors might well feel the convenience and lighter weight on an air-cooled engine would best fit their needs, whilst a more serious cruiser might prefer to go for the quieter, smoother outboard,

Detachable mounting bracket on a Mark IV

as it would more likely to be used for longer periods in little or no wind situations.

Outboard brackets

The outboard can be fitted directly over the transom, though it is advisable to fit pads to reinforce the transom to save the clamps marking the wood or glass fibre. Where an outboard is regularly carried on cruising trips, it is of considerable advantage to fit a removable bracket on the transom. It is then possible to keep the outboard permanently fixed to the bracket whilst sailing, making it readily available when needed. The outboard should always be secured to the boat with a length of line, so that if it is dropped in the water whilst being fitted, or pulled off by the mainsheet hooking underneath it when gybing, it will still be secured to the boat. There are two disadvantages to having the outboard permanently fixed to a bracket on the transom. The first is that of having any weight at the extremities of the boat increases its moment of inertia, and thus decreases boat speed. In this case it is a matter of deciding whether the convenience of having the outboard readily available overrides the very slight disadvantage in performance. The other problem is that of the mainsheet catching on the raised motor, particularly when gybing. There are a number of ways to reduce this possibility:

1. Fitting the outboard on the port side of the transom puts the steering arm - which is always fitted on the engine's port side - as far out of the way as possible, and reduces the chances of mainsheet snagging on this part.

2. Using centre sheeting, and moving the upper pulley some 200mm inboard along the boom will assist in bringing any loose mainsheet inboard.

3. Fitting a length of shockcord, running from one side deck to the other (by the front of the rear locker) and clipping it to, or passing it through, the pulley block on the bridle of a centre mainsheet system, will, with the shockcord tensioned sufficiently, pull the mainsheet inboard whenever there is any slackness in the line. This is probably the most efficient of the methods of preventing the mainsheet snagging the motor.

The outboard can also be clamped to a purpose-made bracket, and fitted directly onto the rudder fittings, in place of the rudder. The main problem with this arrangement is the time it takes to change from the rudder to outboard (or back again), as well as having no control over the steerage of the boat whilst carrying out the operation. There is also the inconvenience of finding somewhere in the boat to carry and store the purpose made bracket when not in use.

Outboard storage
It is possible to store the smaller sized outboards in the back locker, but a more convenient position may be to tie it down in front of the rear locker. With the Wayfarer World, the most convenient place is probably directly aft of the mast, across the centreboard casing.

Outboard steering
The easiest method of steering the boat when using the outboard is to keep the outboard steering friction fairly tight in order to keep the engine straight, and to use the tiller and rudder to steer the boat. Care needs to be taken not to move the tiller over too far; otherwise the prop may catch on the rudder blade. Whenever manoeuvring the boat in a confined space however, it is best to steer with both the outboard and rudder.

Buying an Outboard
Points to look for when buying an outboard are how light it is, how easy it is to carry (ideally it ought to have a carrying handle), how noisy it is, and how much it causes the boat to vibrate when used. A list of suitable current models available can be checked on the website. Small, light, and completely silent electric outboards of approximately 1.5 HP are available on the market, which are ideal for use in rivers, perhaps even estuaries. They are not really powerful enough for use at sea, and are entirely dependent for power and length of time they will operate on the amount of charge in a heavy car type battery.

Towing and Being Towed
The most convenient point to tie the towrope for the boat doing the towing is probably the anchor points for the mainsheet bridle on the transom (where this system is used for a centre mainsheet system), as this helps to keep the line as far from the outboard as possible. Otherwise, the towing rope can be brought through the centre cutout section on the transom for the tiller, and tied or clipped to any convenient strong anchor point. When being towed, it is advisable to pass the rope through a fairlead on the bow (if one is fitted – which is recommended), and wrap it around the mast for a couple of turns, holding onto the end. All the pressure in the towrope will be taken by the turns around the mast, making it easy to keep hold, and the towrope can be immediately released, when necessary. It is advisable to raise the centreboard when being towed. The main problem when towing is the 'snatching', which always occurs in any swell. It is possible to overcome this by making up a towrope of the thickest (10mm) shockcord available, some 5m or more in length. (A small fender secured in the middle will provide sufficient drag to keep the line away from the prop, and a strong clip at one (or both) ends will ensure quick fastening or release). The shockcord is stronger than might be thought, and certainly sufficient for towing more than one Wayfarer. The stretch in the line makes the tow completely smooth, taking out all the stresses on the anchorage points in both boats when any 'snatching' occurs.

Anchors and Anchoring
The two types of anchor recommended for a Wayfarer are the Danforth, and the CQR, with a minimum weight of at least 2.5Kg (5½ lb); anything less may not hold. Both have good general holding power on most types of sea bottom. The Grapnel is probably the most popular type of anchor carried in dinghies, because of its storage convenience, but it is really only effective if used as a shore (kedge) anchor, or in shallow water, where it is possible to bury it in the ground. It is unlikely to hold the boat as a sea (bower) anchor when most needed, i.e. in a strong wind or tide situation. It is always advisable to carry two anchors for sea trips, since this makes anchoring off a shore possible.

A minimum 1m length of chain – weighing around 2Kg is recommended, with at least 30m of anchor line for estuary sailing, and 50m for sea/offshore sailing. It is advisable to use Nylon (or similar material that has a tendency to stretch) for the anchor line, and for this to be wound around a freely rotating drum. The drum needs to be fixed somewhere around the mast tabernacle, either to one side on an elongated mast pin, or under the foredeck immediately behind the mast, (but allowing enough space for the heel of the mast when lowered). Any anchor line that is coiled will inevitably become tangled. An alternative method of storing the anchor line where a drum is not available is to lay it carefully into a bucket. The free end is secured to an anchor point on the boat, and the line is lead hand-over-hand into the bucket until a point near the anchor attachment is reached. The bucket then needs to be secured, so the line stays in place. When needed, the anchor can be dropped overboard without the line becoming tangled.

Anchors should ideally be reasonably accessible, near to the centre of the boat, and as far away from any compass as possible – certainly at least a metre. A useful place to carry a Danforth anchor (for the early Marks of Wayfarers) is under the front seats, with the base clipped to the floorboard. A CQR may be fixed to the front of the centreboard case. Another useful option is secure it to the floor under the thwart, particularly where two anchors are carried. There are a variety of storage solutions used by different cruisers, and the location is largely a matter of personal preference.

Practising beaching on rollers at a cruising conference......

...... and now doing it for real

Beach Landing and using Fenders as Rollers

One of the advantages of Wayfarer cruising is the comparative ease with which it is possible to land on a beach, either temporarily, or to set up a boat or land tent for an overnight stop. There are, however, some advisable precautions to make the landing process go smoothly. If there are heavy breakers pounding the shore, it is totally inadvisable to land. Where there are smaller breaking waves, it is best to lay a sea anchor before reaching the breakers, and either row in, or let the wind blow the boat in, stern first, gradually paying out the anchor line to give some control and prevent either the boat being capsized by the breaking waves, or cause the boat to be crashed sideways onto the shore. Laying an anchor in this way is also a useful way of getting off the shore again with any onshore breeze.

There is usually no difficulty in landing on a beach in normal sailing conditions. The precaution in this situation however, is not to leave the boat on the immediate shoreline, where even the most gentle of ripples on the beach will cause small stones to jam the centreboard. It is always advisable either to anchor the boat in slightly deeper water, or roll the boat up the shoreline beyond the ripples of the tide. Anyone who has not experienced stones jamming the centreboard would be surprised at just how immovable the centreboard can become. It is always advisable to check the centreboard immediately on leaving the beach, (and to stop trying to move it, the moment any resistance is felt). Should there be a problem, the best method of resolving it is either to use a hand pump to pump water down from the top of the centreplate housing to wash the stones out – the same way they came in – or to use a bucket to the same effect. Some experienced cruisers carry a strip of 1mm stainless steel about 35mm wide and 600mm long with a hook cut into the end to pull out the stones from underneath, though this does entail getting the boat ashore, and pulling the mast over to lay the boat on its side, so that the stones can be pulled out from the bottom. Far better to avoid the possibility of getting stones jammed in the centreboard in the first place! Centreboard slot gaskets may help to reduce ingress of sand and stones – they were fitted to some cruising Wayfarers before they were finally legalised for racing.

It is not difficult to roll a Wayfarer up a beach with only two people – although the more people available, the easier it obviously becomes. The process can also be carried out by a single person, using a block and tackle (or the mainsheet or kicking strap blocks) and a long length of suitable line. A sausage type plastic fender is placed under the stern, as the boat is pulled into the shallows backwards. The boat is then rolled on to it until the fender reaches a point around the centreboard housing, when a second fender is placed under the stern. The boat can be rolled up a beach with only two fenders, although three tend to make the job easier, particularly when the fenders start moving off the centre-line of the boat as it is being rolled along.

Plastic fenders need to be large and substantial enough to support a Wayfarer, (usually laden with cruising gear) and roll it up a beach. A minimum size of 150mm diameter, and around 600mm long is recommended. These can be relatively heavy and take up valuable storage space. An alternative is to use inflatable canvas fenders, which are surprisingly strong, but are considerably more expensive.

Bridge Shooting

Bridges can be 'shot', (i.e. without stopping prior to the bridge to lower the mast), in any sort of following wind. The boat does need some setting up to do this efficiently, but as the system can also make rigging the boat easier, it can be useful to incorporate this into the basic boat set-up as follows:

1. Make the forestay the same length as the shrouds, and attach a long length of line that can be led back to the cockpit. Attach a small block to the bow fitting on the foredeck, through which the forestay line is passed, and then back to a cleat situated at any convenient point for the

crew/helm. This allows the forestay to be released quickly and easily, tensioned whenever necessary, and also speeds rigging the boat when the mast needs to be stepped.

2. Fit a quick release system at the mast end of the kicking strap. The quick release hook/clip will need to have considerable strength; and the greater the loading on the kicking strap system, the more substantial the hook/clip will need to be. Fitting the clip to the lower, rather than upper end of the kicking strap, will keep the kicker system clear of the mast foot area when the mast is being lowered, and moving within the tabernacle.

3. Fit low profile halyard cleats (from Selden Masts) on each side of the mast, (preferably as near to the luff track as possible and close to the boom, or alternatively, below the level of the foredeck, so as to prevent the jib sheets snagging on them). Any other cleating system to keep the jib and main halyards taut may also be used in order to prevent these lines getting caught under the mast foot when the mast is being raised after shooting the bridge. It is always best to practise mast lowering first, without having any bridge to negotiate. Even when approaching a bridge, it is advisable to check the mast is free by lowering it a little way and putting it back up again, whilst there is still time to turn into the bank if something is not right. Having made these checks, the sequence for bridge shooting is as follows:

1. Start organising everything well before the bridge is approached, particularly if new to the procedure, or it is the first of a sequence of bridges.

2. Loosen and detach the kicking strap from the foot of the mast (clipping it onto the boom fitting can keep it tidily out of the way, and prevent it getting caught up on other parts of the boat).

3. If a spinnaker halyard is led back from the mast foot (it is assumed that bridge shooting is not being attempted flying a spinnaker!!) uncleat or loosen the spinnaker halyard so that it doesn't prevent the mast pivoting backwards. Also make sure the spinnaker boom uphaul/ downhaul system will not interfere with the mast being lowered.

4. If approaching under full main, remove the boom from the gooseneck; uncleat and loosen the forestay line; release the genoa halyard from the tensioning device used on the boat; lower the mast a little way to check everything is free, and return the mast to its original position. Leave the forestay loose, and hold on to the genoa halyard, keeping it under tension. All should now be ready to shoot the bridge. The more familiar you get with the sequence, the closer you can get to the bridge before starting the preparations – but it is unwise to become overconfident!

5. Depending on the strength of the wind and the speed of the boat, lower the mast as the bridge is approached, (or in light winds, just before the mast touches the bridge). The mast can be supported by the crew; by the helm on his shoulder; or more conveniently for a longer bridge, by a mast crutch, taking care not to damage the sail. This will leave the crew free to use a paddle should this become necessary.

6. Once clear of the bridge, use the mast cleats to ensure all the halyards are taut and are not likely to foul the mast foot, before starting to raise the mast. The mast can then be physically lifted to start the mast raising process whilst pulling on the genoa halyard to keep it under tension, and completed by re-fitting the genoa halyard onto the tensioning device.

7. Fit the boom back in the gooseneck; clip the kicking strap to the foot of the mast and tension as necessary; then tension the forestay line; and continue sailing.

The above procedure is only suitable with a following wind. If the wind is strong, or sailing near to gybing, it is advisable to take the main down altogether, and sail under genoa/jib only. If the wind is virtually on the nose, then it is better to go to the most windward bank, lower the mast, and pull, paddle, row, or motor under the bridge.

Points to watch:
1. There appear to be very few Wayfarers still using a foresail with a rope luff and jib hanks. However should this be the case, it is necessary to unclip the bottom 2 or 3 jib hanks to prevent them being pulled off as the mast is lowered. It is recommended that this type of foresail be replaced with one with a wire luff and an effective tensioning device, which will dramatically improve the boat's performance, particularly to windward.

2. Remember that when the mast is lowered, it increases the boat's length by around 4m (12ft.), so be aware of possible obstacles and other craft, as well as any current, which could carry the boat into colliding with them.

3. It is always useful to have a paddle or oar handy should any additional speed be necessary for steerage – as well as being useful for fending the boat off obstacles or other craft, should this prove necessary.

Towpath Hauling

Pulling a Wayfarer along a towpath using only the painter is entirely inefficient, since it will cause the bow to be constantly pulled into the bank, even if there is someone steering with the tiller. There are two effective ways of hauling the boat along a riverbank or canal. The first is to combine the painter with a second line attached to a nearside point at the stern. The boat can be kept travelling parallel to the bank by adjusting the pull on each length of line, without anyone needing to be aboard to steer. The second method is to attach a line to the spinnaker halyard, and use this to pull the boat along, with the crew using the tiller to steer. Since the pull on the line is nearer to the centre of the boat, the crew on the tiller can overcome any tendency for the boat to be pulled into the bank. This is a particularly useful method where there are obstacles such as moored motorboats or bushes on the bank to negotiate.

Boat Tents

A boat tent is a great asset for cruising enthusiasts, since there are often occasions where it is not possible to use a land tent. The Association currently has two frame tents for hire to members. These can be particularly useful to newcomers, who can try them out to see how boat tenting suits them, before committing themselves to buying one. Each is available for a hire charge (reduced for UKWA rallies), with a small additional cost of sending it on to the next hirer. The hire tents come with all the fittings needed, and do not require any fixing points to be made in the boat. Anyone interested in purchasing a tent, or making their own, after perhaps trying out one of the Association tents, can obtain more information from the

Frame tent on Bob Harland's Mk1 Woody W7658 Septimus Fry showing front and side access arrangements

UKWA Website. There are three patterns of tents available: the simple boom tent (an inverted V shape); the framed boom tent (inverted U shape); and the framed box tent. Common to all three types will be opening access flaps at the bow and stern. Side door(s), offering easier access in some situations, are usually available as an option. Velcro is normally used as the quickest and easiest fastening method.

Mark 1 (boom tent/inverted V shape)

This is the cheapest, quickest and easiest to erect and is supported by the boom on a stern crutch. The headroom however is somewhat restricted and the only comfortable area for sitting is on the floor in front of the stern locker.

Mark 2 (boom tent/inverted U shape)

This is similar to the Mark 1, except that tent poles or sail battens are used to push out the sides to give sufficient additional space to be able to sit on the side benches a little more comfortably.

Mark 3 (frame tent)

This has a rear framework, (which can be carried behind the rear seats and floorboards on all versions except the SD, World and Mk IV), supporting the boom and 2 poles (oars may alternatively be used), which forms the roof of the tent. This provides more headroom and considerably greater comfort, particularly if having to stay in the tent for longer periods due to bad weather. It takes rather longer to set up, and it is advisable to practise setting this type of tent up at home prior to doing so on the water. Instructions are obviously provided with any new tent supplied, as well as the Association hire tents.

Frank Dye's Wayfarer 'Wanderer' shows off the simplicity of the Mark 1 type tent which is supported by a boom crutch

Charles Ferrar's tent using flexible battens on a Mk IV

Windows
Windows are not essential if a light coloured fabric is used for the tent. A window at the bow can be useful when at anchor. Side windows in a box tent help to reduce the feeling of motion if the boat is swinging at anchor, but are of less use in a boom tent, since they are inclined upwards.

Extended bow
The bow section of the frame tent is normally made to fit around the apex of the washboard. Whilst extending the front section to the bow of the boat can provide useful additional covered storage space on the foredeck, it is generally a disadvantage to have the front of the tent extending this far, since working space on the foredeck is almost essential. When moored 'bow on' to any landing point for example, the front part of the tent will need to be trodden on to gain access inside the tent.

Raised boom
Additional headroom can be achieved by lifting the boom higher. The stern end can be raised using a taller boom crutch, whilst the mast end can be raised in a number of ways. Older boats have masts with a sliding gooseneck that can conveniently achieve this, but the boom can also be lifted with the spinnaker or jib halyard – and the cunningham, or luff reefing line used to secure the boom to the mast, or a modified plastic rowlock used to provide a temporary gooseneck. The main drawback of the higher tent is the considerably greater windage, noticeable in even moderate winds.

The boat tent as an awning
It is often useful to fold the tent back from the stern of the boat to provide more space at the rear, whilst still providing some shelter, particularly when the wind direction is from the bow. With a frame tent, the sides may be rolled up to provide a sunshade – on the odd occasion during the British summer when protection is needed from the sun!

Choice of fabrics
There is a basic choice of a cotton proofed canvas, or a PVA/polyester material. The canvas is cheaper, but heavier. It is generally worth getting a tent made from the lighter, PVA/polyester (Ventile) material since any wetness (which is almost inevitable from early morning dew), will increase the weight of either material, but the weight increase will be noticeably greater in the heavier canvas material. Tents are best made from a light, or pastel colour, which gives a feeling of airiness and reduces the time that the tent has to be illuminated, particularly if cruising during the darker nights of Autumn. Tents made with dark coloured material tend to make the inside dark and somewhat dismal, and too bright a colour can lead to an unpleasant 'fluorescent' effect. Most materials come in a choice of colours, although the lightweight PVA/polyester is generally only available in olive green and dark blue.

Anne Kell's frame tent on W247 Emma - shown here tied up at Woodbridge

Cooking Stoves
Most cruisers normally only prepare relatively simple meals, though it has been known for more elaborate dishes to be cooked. To describe more on preparing foods is outside the scope of this book, but the subject is often covered at each year's Wayfarer Cruising Conference, where it is possible to keep up with the latest developments. There are a number of stoves available, which burn various fuels. The following are the most common and popular:

Paraffin stoves
The most familiar of this type of stove is the 'Primus'. It burns with a very hot flame, but needs a separate priming fuel – usually methylated spirit (meths), to heat the burner to a sufficient temperature to cause the vaporised paraffin to ignite. They tend to be rather bulky, and need to be shielded from draughts; with a little practice usually being needed to get them started using the meths primer. Flaring can occur during the lighting operation and the jet must be kept clean. Paraffin is easy to obtain, and inexpensive. Spilled fuel will not ignite easily, but doesn't evaporate quickly, and tends to leave a lingering smell.

Butane/Propane gas cylinders

A butane gas burner is simple to use and gives instant heat output. Replacement cartridges are easy to obtain but the overall cost of the fuel is considerably greater than paraffin. It is inefficient when not shielded from draughts, and the heat output diminishes as the fuel is used up. The gas will explode if ignited after being allowed to leak from the container and mix with air in confined spaces, including a boat or land tent – there have been incidents of this happening with serious consequences. Cartridges therefore need to be changed outside of any tent.

Methylated spirits

This stove is commonly known as a Trangia, after the Swedish firm that makes them. It burns the meths without the need for it to be pressurised. They are easy to light, and quiet, but the flame temperature is lower than with the other liquid fuels. The whole unit of 2 saucepans, a lid, handle, stove, matches or lighter, and a small container of spare fuel can all be contained within the whole unit, and is hence usefully compact for storing in a Wayfarer. The Trangia is ideal for boiling water for tea, coffee and either cooking, or heating up pre-packed simple meals. The fuel is more expensive than paraffin but spilled meths will evaporate quickly, leaving no smell.

Sleeping Aboard

Space for sleeping aboard a Wayfarer can be somewhat restricted, particularly in Wayfarer Marks up to the 'World' design. For these earlier Marks, there is a choice of either sleeping on the floorboards, with the feet beneath the thwart, or on the side benches, normally made temporarily wider with slats of wood. Sleeping on the floorboards has the disadvantage of considerable restriction of legroom beneath the thwart, and the boat also has to be set up (if hauled out of the water), to ensure the stern is higher than the bow, since it is not comfortable to sleep when the head level is lower than the feet. If this is the preferred option for sleeping, then it is usually advisable to remove the rear seats permanently. Where the rear seats are considered to be a more comfortable option for cruising, then there is the possibility of temporarily widening the front and rear seats (cruisers have come up with various ways of doing this) to create a wider sleeping area. Using this option has the disadvantage of taking longer to set the boat up for the night, but the advantage of offering no restriction of leg room, a choice of which way round to sleep, and a useful storage area beneath the seats. The 'World' and latest Mk IV versions of Wayfarer offer a much greater length of floor space for sleeping – providing the auxiliary rear locker is not used, or removed – which gives a considerably greater degree of comfort at night.

Where the boat has been hauled out for an overnight stop on a beach, it is helpful to arrive around high tide, in order to be left 'high and dry' for most of the night asleep. It is advisable to ensure the anchor(s) are secure as the tide goes out, placing fenders under the boat to prevent it rocking, (and always attached to the boat with a line to prevent them floating away

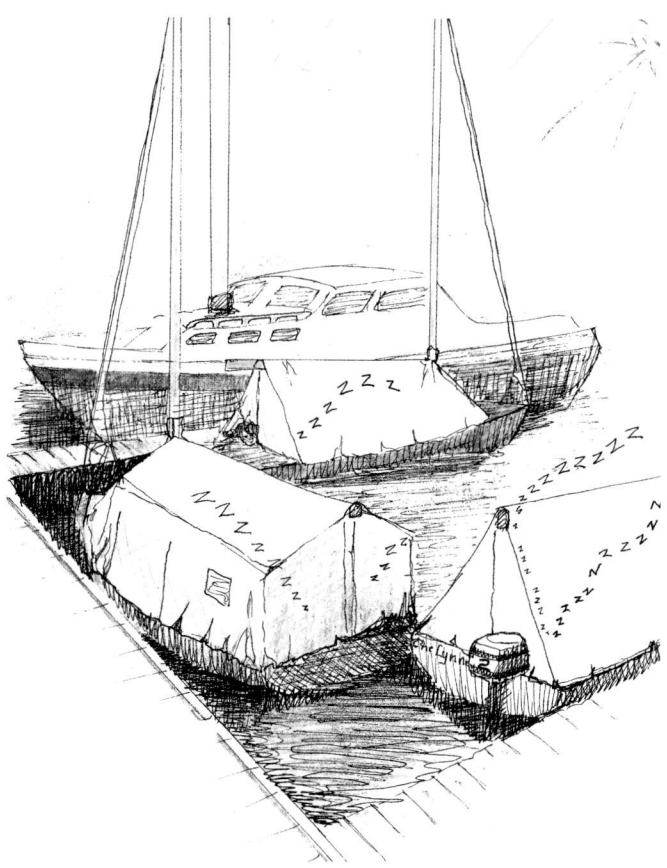

Overnight stop at Woodbridge - "Are you asleep?"

on the next incoming tide). When the tide does come back in, it is possible to rest peacefully, knowing that everything is perfectly secure, and if necessary, use the anchor line to pull the boat out into deeper water as the tide ebbs, in order to save rolling the boat down the beach to launch. When moored at a marina or alongside a jetty or other fixture, large blow-up fenders offer the best possible protection, but two or more strategically placed large plastic fenders also perform perfectly well. It is always worth wrapping halyards around the shrouds wherever the boat is situated for an overnight stop, to prevent them slapping against the mast in a breeze.

It is recommended that the best quality sleeping bag that can be afforded be purchased, since nothing will make a cruise more miserable than being too cold to sleep properly. A sleeping bag with at least a 3 season grading is recommended, and it is worth considering the weight factor when making a purchase, since the even small amounts of additional weight can mount up to make a significant difference. A pillow can be made up from an item or two of clothing, or a spinnaker. A closed cell foam camper mat can be used on its own as a mattress, but a considerably more comfortable night's sleep can be obtained by using a good quality self-inflating mattress. Most cruisers feel that a self-inflating mattress is well worth the investment, but since it is important that these aren't punctured, it is worth combining it with a camper mat, and first placing the mat on the deck floor to afford the mattress some protection from sand, grit, and any sharp edges.

A CRUISE TO A BLACKWATER RALLY - AND BACK

There are many cruising logs available as pdf files on the Wayfarer website. Many are also first presented in the UKWA Wayfarer News. This is an example to illustrate some of the points made in this chapter. Anne Kell (W247 Emma) describes a passage from the River Orwell made in May 2009 to join up with a Blackwater Rally and wonderfully illustrates the decision making process involving time, tide and weather forecasts.

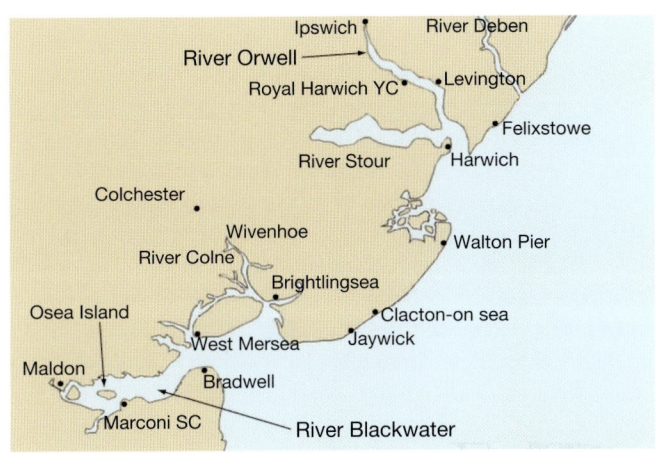

Deliberations - should you believe the forecast? The eagerly awaited Wayfarer News landed on the mat and before long I was poring over the rally details for the coming year. Great, a rally on my doorstep, within sailing distance and with the added bonus of being in the school holidays, so no panic about being back for work the next day. Date in the diary, rally organiser notified; now all I have to do is wait on the forecast. The River Orwell to the River Blackwater necessitates an open sea passage of about 25 miles along a fairly exposed stretch of the North Sea coast, with few bolt holes, so the weather becomes a major determining factor. In the week leading up to the rally I kept a careful eye on the developing forecasts and all boded well for the week ahead. South Westerlies were forecast, so that means a beat all the way, but generally the wind strength was ideal for a Wayfarer with force 3 to 4 predicted for the coming few days. Sadly, a change in wind direction to NE for the return trip may mean yet another a beat along the Essex coast – ah well, that's the luck of the draw. Now to check on the tides. The organisers had done their homework and picked ideal tides for their cruise. A rising tide on the Saturday morning meant taking the flood from the Marconi Sailing Club at Stansgate up to Maldon for lunch and then back to Brightlingsea on the ebb for the first planned overnight stop. Unfortunately for us, sailing down from the north to join the other participants on the rally, the timings were not so ideal. To make full use of the rising tide going south would necessitate a very early morning start, so we decided to try and gain some time by setting off on Friday evening and making our way down river to the mouth at Harwich, where we would pick up a buoy or lie to anchor over night, ready to catch the first of the rise in the morning.

So much for the planning …….
Despite all our advance planning and pre-packing, by the time we had escaped work on the Friday, picked up all our gear, loaded up the boat and launched it was already 7 o'clock. We knew we would have to buck the tide on the Orwell but with a fair wind that was easily possible. The key words to note here are 'fair wind'! The forecast for 7 p.m. Friday evening was F2 – 3. The actual wind was more like F1 – 2 and dropping. After an hour we had covered 1.5 miles and the oars were out. After 2 hours we had made Levington, about 3 miles short of our intended destination. As the light was going we decided to pick up the nearest buoy, erected the boat tent and set the alarm for 3 a.m! After all the forecast for Saturday was good, a gentle F3 predicted; we can still make it, even if we only meet the fleet at Brightlingsea in the evening.

Three a.m. dawns – well not quite dawns, it is still dark! With a rapid turn around we are ready to leave by 4 a.m. having converted our 'home' back into a 'sailing dinghy'. We're off ….. and rowing. Two hours and 5 miles later we are still rowing. Brightlingsea seems an awful long way off. But the tide is now in our favour. Ahead we can see the smallest of ripples forming on the water; spirits lifted, this looks promising. Within half an hour there is sufficient wind to ship the oars and raise the main – we're sailing! We can make it! Now the Gods have obviously taken pity on us and decided to reward us for our determination not to be beaten by the lack of wind; it's an easterly (so much for weather forecasts) – wonderful, no beating! We have a cracking sail, reaching all the way along the Essex coast past the two piers of Walton and Clacton and round into the Blackwater. With the bonus of a 1.5 knot spring tide under us and a favourable F3 becoming 4 wind we are making 6 knots and the sun is shining. By the time we get to Bradwell, not only is meeting the fleet looking a distinct possibility but we may also make it to Maldon to join them for lunch. At 1200 we land by Maldon promenade just as the fleet of 10 other Wayfarers are preparing to leave. We have covered 35 miles in 8 hours, including 2.5 hours of rowing. Just enough time to rush to the kiosk, grab a bag of chips and a cup of tea, and we are off again, this time sailing in company.

Mark 1 woody W247 'Emma' reaches Wivenhoe

We cross the causeway south of Northey Island and then have a brief stop on the north end of Osea Island. At this point we discover that one of the fleet has broken its rudder after an argument with the mud and is heading back to Marconi S.C. for a replacement. The rest of the Wayfarer fleet jills around in the middle of the channel awaiting their return and watches the spectacle of a massive fleet of juniors racing in Cadets – possibly 2012 beckons for some of them. Listening in on the VHF makes for added entertainment. First attempt at a start - "We're going to have to have a general recall." Second attempt - "They're playing games with us." Third attempt "It's easier to say which boats aren't over the line!" The wind is now in the south, F3, so we make good progress with an ebbing tide down river towards Brightlingsea. It always seems to take an eternity to cross Mersea Flats and here we have to put in the first tacks of the day to avoid the shallows. Those with local knowledge 'steal a march' on those more worried about finding the bottom but soon the whole fleet is safely moored against the mid river pontoons. Emma has covered 51 miles in the day. Two crews opted to sleep on board, ourselves included, while the rest ferry their gear ashore and make for the local campsite, 5 minutes walk from the hard. A pleasant evening is spent in good company in the local pub.

Sunday dawns bright but windless. However, we are confident that the sea breeze will arrive by mid-morning and the fleet makes a leisurely start, this time heading up the River Colne towards Rowhedge. After a frustrating drift, a gentle breeze fills in and we have a lovely run up the river. Most of the fleet stops at Rowhedge for lunch while two Wayfarers -yes, you guessed it, Emma included - decide to see how far up the Colne they can get. Having reached the industrial outskirts of Colchester we call it a day and turn around. The beat back is reminiscent of sailing on the Broads, frantic tight turns making the most of the lift gained on each bank. The wind picks up for the afternoon and we have an exciting beat back, first to Stone Point on the end of Mersea Island, and then back to our pontoon berth at Brightlingsea. We regrouped in an 'interesting' pub, complete with its own home brew and 'larger than life' landlord. Sunday night was to be decision time for us. We would have to sail back to the Orwell sometime over the next two days and everything was dependent on that forecast. Sunday night's forecast gave N veering NE 3-4 (i.e. on the nose all the way home) for the next 24 hours, with E/NE becoming W/NW 3-4 for Tuesday but thunderstorms later. If we could miss the thunderstorms I preferred the sound of the W/NW over the E/NE. Maybe Tuesday would be the day for the return trip and we could sail with the fleet on the final day of their cruise.

What a difference a night makes. Monday morning's forecast gave E 3-4, backing NW 4-5 becoming cyclonic 5-7 later with thunderstorms. And for the Tuesday – NW backing SW F4-5 increasing to F6. Just where did that wind suddenly come from? So our plans changed again; if we can beat the 5-7 and thunderstorms we'll be OK but we will have to leave sooner rather than later and that means an unfavourable tide as well as wind direction. Still on a positive note, with them both in the same direction the sea state shouldn't be too bad!!!

We say our farewells and thanks to the organisers and set off at about 1000. We had a fast reach out of the Colne, round Colne Point and put in our first reef. Beating against the tide is slow progress and we are only making about 2.5 nm/hour in the direction we want to go i.e. NE. Despite our ideas to the contrary, the sea state is decidedly lumpy and the crew is getting wet (not good for morale). Our force 4 becomes a force 5, gusting 6 and the seas are getting bigger and the boat wetter. Emma rides the waves and crashes down the other side, sending shivers through her timbers and bringing her to a halt in the troughs, as there is no time to react to the short chop. If this is what it is like when wind is with tide, what will it be like in an hour's time when the tide turns? Off Jaywick are a series of Y shaped groynes put in to try and reduce erosion. We decide to tuck in behind one of these to take stock. After a welcome cup of coffee and no obvious change in the sea state, we decide we have no option but to turn around and run under jib back towards Brightlingsea. It takes us an hour to cover the ground we have won so hard over the previous two. All the time we are deliberating about the chances of sailing home versus the need to go and collect the car and trailer and where would be the best place to recover, given that we would need to use public transport to get back to Ipswich and home.

Then there is a glimmer of hope. The wind is dropping and the sun is coming out. We put up the main, two reefs, and then in rapid succession only one and then none at all. Full sail and a comfortable ride. We are virtually back to where we had started from, just off Colne Point. 'Let's give it another try.' So its back to beating north covering the same ground again. This time we head out into The Wallet to make the most of the tide, which has now turned in our favour, and go to visit the new construction site of wind turbines being erected on the Gunfleet Sands. Despite the fears of wind against tide, the sea state is now relatively calm and we make excellent progress in a NE 3-4. What a difference a bit of sun makes as well. By 1600 we are off Walton Pier and the mouth of the Orwell is in sight. What a relief!

Brewing up to the east of us are the promised thunder clouds with their anvil shaped tops. As we round Harwich we have our first crack of lightning and rumble of thunder – still 5 miles off fortunately. But now the wind starts to drop (so much for the F5-7 later). Our progress slows and once again the tide is against us up the river. It is only 1800 but it feels like 2100 with leaden skies, and then the rain starts. At low water we reach the Royal Harwich, our home club. Sadly, the lack of water means we can't retrieve the boat, so we tie her up against the pontoons and abandon her for the night to seek out a hot bath and a nice comfortable bed. So, just how much can you rely on the forecast? I suppose, at the end of the day, it is only a best guess and you just have to be prepared to modify your plans accordingly. We did the right thing in the end as Tuesday saw strong winds, as promised, and rain!

THE SOUND OF JURA
A THREE ISLAND CRUISE

In another taster John Mellor summarises his June 2005 trip to the Western Isles of Scotland

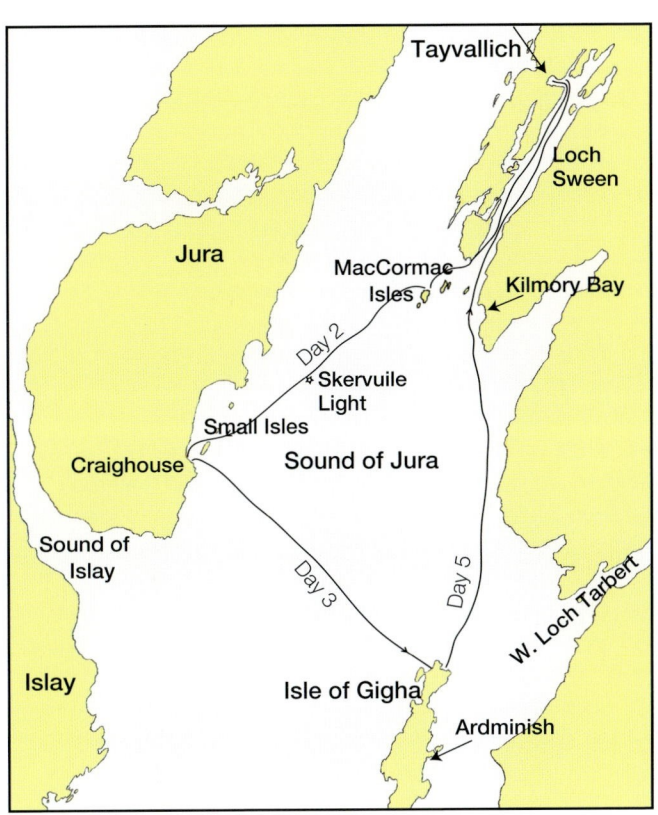

Having day-sailed on the west coast of Scotland for a number of years it was time for a cruise. A winter of planning and calculating led to a cruise programme that would take us from Tayvallich at the head of Loch Sween to the Isle of Jura and then on to the island of Colonsay and back. A four-day trip for which if we allowed a week then there should be time to allow for the vagaries of the weather. We ended up with two boats on the cruise. Vera, fresh from her day skipper shore based navigation course, would be my crew in my World W10053 and Cedric and Chris would be in Cedric's Mark II W7424. Tayvallich is a long way from our homes, it takes about two and a half hours from Glasgow, and so Saturday was spent driving there. Leachive Campsite is well positioned for a view over Tayvallich Bay and next to the pub, which serves good food, mostly locally caught seafood. With the tides as they were, we needed to arrive at the MacCormac Isles in time to take the south going tidal stream at 4.30 pm (south going stream +05.45 GMT Dover). We decided on a leisurely crack of noon start and with a light northerly wind it made for a very

Mark 1 Woody W175 at Kilmory Beach
- The Paps of Jura in the distance.

easy sail south down Loch Sween with the wind behind us. About half way down Loch Sween the wind died away and then swung round to the south and freshened up a bit. This made for a very pleasant series of long tacks with both crews sat on the side decks. According to the Pilot most of the dangers in the sound of Jura are congregated round the MacCormac Isles and the chart also warns of strong tidal streams. With our arrival timed to coincide with the change of tide we experienced no problems. The anchorage on the MacCormac Isles is well protected and our Wayfarers were able to tuck into the side, next to a stone landing place on the west of the anchorage. The water here is deep enough for a Wayfarer to stay afloat at all states of the tide. It is also lovely and clear and whilst we did not see any fish there were plenty of other creatures to look at. We explored the island and visited an old chapel and the cave where St. Cormack lived. From the high point of the island, where there is a Celtic cross, we got a good view of the tide races round the island. It was also the place where a week later I was to see two otters playing in the rock pools and in amongst the yellow flag irises. It was such a nice evening that we decided to stay where we were for the night rather than journey on to Jura. We could have made it by 9pm given that the wind held but it could just have easily dropped. We were there, after all, to enjoy the trip and staying put would allow more breathing time for the Shiraz.

That night it rained; boy did it rain. The new untried tent decided to leak just above my head, which as Vera pointed out was not a problem on her side. Did I get wet?? Not at all. I had the foresight to be snug in my Goretex bivi bag. A huge affair bought from an army surplus supplier. It is big enough to get all of me and all my kit inside and with it pulled up over my head I slept quite dry. The next morning saw me in a puddle of water. But I was still dry. What a great bit of kit. Monday dawned brightish and we set off to Craighouse which is situated on the southeast corner of Jura with the Small Isles protecting it. Off we set, and as soon as we rounded the corner of the Island we were into the first tide race. With wind against tide it made for a bit of a bumpy start. The wind was southerly; mainly force three, occasionally four. With the GPS reading about 6mph we made Craighouse in one beat. Not

"I Know I said 'shorten sail' - but I meant you to reef"

that it was an easy ride. Our course was set to pass north of Skervuile light, which protects ships from some shallow water and Beloe rock. Skervuile light is a tall (22m) white pillar. Knowing that the tide was under us also meant that we would be getting close to Skervuile light so we had to keep a good watch. We didn't see anything but Cedric and Chris caught sight of a rock. With the shallow water and wind against tide we were expecting a bit of a chop and we weren't disappointed. "Wow, look behind at Cedric," I said to Vera after a particularly big swoosh off and down a wave. "Not yet", exclaimed Vera, "Hang on". It was at this point that we started to get bruised bums. Glancing behind at Cedric and Chris you could see some great photographs in the making with spray shooting up and over their boat. With two hands needed for the boat the chance of a photograph was slim. "How big were the waves?" Vera was later to ask. I said about three or four foot to which Vera replied "Oh yes? More like ten foot." Did I say that this was only the second Wayfarer sea cruise that Vera had done? I didn't want to put her off. Approaching The Small Isles we aimed at the most northerly gap between the islands but with the tide behind us we ended up in the third gap not the first. Once inside the islands, the sea calmed and the sun came out and warmed us. There is a small boat harbour just below the distillery with a nice sandy beach so we pulled up on to it and went seeking refreshments at the local hotel. The hotel caters for visiting sailors by providing shower and toilet facilities to the rear. We stopped for coffee and lunch and tea at the hotel. Well it was a nice day so we went for a walk. The lawn in front of the hotel is just wonderful. Lovely views over the bay and waiter service. Not only this but the hotel allows people to camp on its lawn. The charge: a donation in the bar. Talking to other sailors

CRUISING GUIDE & STRATEGIES

that evening (big boats and paid skippers) it was amusing to see their reactions to our cruise in such little boats.

The plan for Tuesday was to sail through the Sound of Islay and then onwards to Colonsay. We awaited the weather forecast. Variable three to five and perhaps southerly five to seven for the following day. This was a bad forecast for us so a change of plan was called for. Cedric favoured sailing back across the Sound of Jura and a bit further south to the island of Gigha. We all agreed. Typically this was the large-scale chart I hadn't bought; after all we wouldn't be going there. Tuesday brought bright sunny weather with a light northerly breeze. Charts, protractor, GPS, rulers, pencils, tide tables and much calculating later I heard myself saying "Just head south east". Which is just what we did. The wind by now was very light, more like a drift than a sail. The sun beat down and everyone was vying for position in the shade of the sail. It was a long sail from mid-morning to teatime but we didn't mind. The views were lovely; we saw porpoises and a good variety of birds. We approached Gigha as the wind started to pick up a bit. We were heading for a bay on the northwest tip of Gigha, a perfect bit of white sandy beach with good protection from the forecast southerly wind. The next day, Wednesday, was a grey day. We had hoped to rejuvenate last night's bonfire for our morning toast but we were greeted with a damp morose whiff of smoke so back to the fruesli bars and fruit. Since we had reached Gigha we decided to have a look at the island by circumnavigating it. The wind was light to start with but as we headed south down the west coast of Gigha it started to pick up and it wasn't long before we started to get waves breaking over the foredeck. The newly planted spray decks on the World now came into their own. Instead of the water running across the deck and depositing itself in the cockpit it hit the beautifully oiled wood, rose up a couple of feet, hit us in the face and then went in the cockpit. The compensation was the knowledge that the spray deck was really for the boat tent to fit properly. On we sailed down the coast of Gigha. The fine mist and rain meant we couldn't get much of a view but the sailing was good. The wind and rain continued to build up. As we turned the bottom end of the Island the waves were breaking continuously and with the wind now behind us it made for a swift run. The main village on Gigha, Ardminish, is situated on the east coast and according to the pilot there is a cafe and landing place to the south of the ferry terminal. "Shall we stop for coffee?" I asked. A silly question really. I'm sure I would have had a mutiny on my hands if we hadn't stopped. By now the wind was building up behind us and so I decided not to reef the mainsail but to drop it completely. Our speed dropped a bit but we were still doing six knots with just the genoa. The village of Ardminish bay started to open out on our left and being careful to pass north of the red can buoy we reached in towards shore where we found a small sandy beach and a closed cafe. Needing to stretch our legs anyway we went in search of the Hotel. Gigha seems to be getting geared up for the yachties - the bar of the hotel has a stone floor to cater for the damp customers. After coffee there was talk of continuing up the sound of Jura and going to Lagg bay on Jura but in the end we decided to head for a small bay on the north east tip of Gigha.

This night was quite stormy so all four of us spent the evening in the World, which without the rear locker is quite spacious. Cedric supplied the canapés and the rest of us supplied the wine. After being buffeted all night our bay was relatively quiet the next morning. Looking out into the Sound of Gigha was a different story. White caps covered the whole area so we knew what to expect. We were to head north with a southerly wind so both boats set two reefs in the main and Cedric put up his small headsail. We set off with Chris and Cedric leading the way across the sound of Gigha towards West Loch Tarbet. This wasn't too bad with the wind on the starboard quarter. Fast but in control. The roller furling on my boat came into its own on as it enabled me to keep station on Cedric by furling or letting out sail as necessary. I didn't fancy gybing as we neared the shore. Neither did Chris so we both wore round to take the wind directly behind us. Goose-winged in a strong wind is not my favourite point of sailing and while Vera whooped as we surfed down the waves I was more concerned in watching out for the rogue wave or wind shift that could promote an unplanned gybe. After a couple of hours we got some shelter in the entrance to Loch Sween, where we gybed and headed up the loch. Not too far along the loch, Castle Sween caravan site provided respite where we had lunch and a pot of coffee in the bar. before running up the Loch to Tayvallich. I went up the left hand side of the loch whilst Chris opted for the right hand side. "Why are they going up the wrong side in other words the longest way?" asked Vera. "Watch", I replied. Sure enough as we reached the turning point to head towards the village Chris rounded up and raised full sail for a flat out reach to journey's end. A great idea, but just like so many of our plans this trip, he was to be foiled as the wind dropped and we cruised gently up to Tayvallich jetty.

COMFORT & SAFETY ZONE

Personal Buoyancy

It is strongly recommended that personal buoyancy be worn at all times. The international standard EN ISO 12402 series is intended to classify and cover the complete range of personal flotation devices (PFD) available. ISO 12402-5 refers to 50 Newton devices intended for use by swimmers in sheltered waters with help at hand. This is the standard normally used for dinghy sailors where there is safety boat cover. There are more devices in the series; ISO 12402-4 refers to 100N inland/inshore life jackets and so on up to ISO 12402-2 which provides buoyancy, or effective upward force, of 275 Newtons to the average wearer, making the product more likely to keep the wearer's face out of the water in rough offshore conditions. Unfortunately, the higher Newton garments may be bulky to wear, particularly around the front of the body, causing some restriction of movement – an important consideration when dealing with a capsize - the most likely reason for being in the water and needing personal buoyancy. They also offer little protection against the cold to the upper body whilst in the water – hypothermia being a much more likely cause of death than drowning. If protective headgear is worn to help prevent being knocked unconscious, the lower category buoyancy aids are likely to offer a greater degree of overall safety than full life jackets.

Self-inflating Life Jackets

Self-inflating life jackets overcome the problem of the bulkiness and the restricted movement allowed by the normal life jacket, as they are inflated automatically (or manually) only when in the water. Unfortunately, this still means they offer restricted movement once in the water. An incident has occurred where a Wayfarer sailor, whose life jacket of this type didn't immediately inflate after capsizing, eventually became so cold that assistance was needed to inflate it, and he subsequently required hospital treatment to recover from hypothermia. It is also worth being aware that a self-inflating lifejacket can create a dangerous situation if the wearer is underneath an inverted boat.

Clothing

It is vitally important when sailing to wear sufficient and adequate clothing to keep warm and dry in the prevailing conditions. It is also necessary - particularly when cruising - to take additional layers to put on should conditions deteriorate. Spare base and mid-layer clothing should be carried in a dry bag securely fastened in the cockpit of the boat. After a capsize and recovery it is important to have dry, warm clothing to hand and not in a locker. It is essential even when sailing in the hottest, mildest conditions that a wind and waterproof outer garment is either worn or at least available in the boat. Conditions out on the water, and particularly at sea, can be vastly different to those experienced on land, and can also change very rapidly. Wet suits work by initially providing a good layer of insulation between the body and cold water, and when wet, trapping a layer of water between the body and the wet suit, which warms to body temperature and gives further insulation. Because the body tends to stay wet, often from perspiration, if not from immersion in water, wet suits are not particularly comfortable to wear for long periods, and are therefore not generally favoured by cruisers. If you are cruising for a few hours whilst wearing a "wet" wet suit, you will get cold. They will however be more effective if worn under a windproof one-piece suit or outer jacket and trousers.

Dry suits may be worn over the top of normal clothing, but wicking polyester or quality fleece make better under-layers. A dry suit has latex seals at the neck, wrists and ankles to make the suit watertight. Care needs to be taken to expel air from the suit after fitting, since on immersion, it is possible for the air trapped in the legs of the suit to unbalance the support provided by the personal buoyancy. Any perspiration is obviously trapped within the suit if it is a non-breathable one. It should be noted that dry suits require wet suit (or similar) boots to be worn in order to protect the dry suit material at the feet. An alternative to the dry suit, particularly for cruisers and day sailors, is the modern 'breathable' type of clothing, with trade names of 'Trax' and 'Buffalo'. The garments are somewhat more expensive, but very effective at keeping the body warm. They are designed to wick perspiration away from the body, a feature essential for inner body warmth. Wearing this type of clothing for occasions where immersion into the water is unlikely, only an inner layer, and mid layer (or two), together with suitable outer weatherproof protection, is all that is necessary for even quite harsh conditions.

Keeping the head warm in cold conditions is vital, as this is where the body loses a lot of heat. Fleece or fleece-lined hats are good, especially if they are waterproof and have earflaps and a peak. Sun hats in summer to protect the head, neck and ears combined with sun block and lip salve can save you from a lot of pain. There are many types of glove on the market and each has their own merits. Leather sailing gloves will protect you from chafe if you are doing a lot of sail adjusting. Dry gloves can help prolong the sailing season.

What not to wear? Cotton tee shirts are out, as is any cotton garment. Once wet, they stay wet and cold. Look out for polyester and polartec clothing, or choose an integrated clothing system. When cruising, you will find you need much warmer clothing than you think. A summer cruise can see you wearing base and fleece mid-layer clothing, covered by a set of foul weather waterproofs - these can soon be shed for shorts and tee shirt on reaching the beach!

Well togged up at a Brancaster Ladies' Rally in January 2006! Also shows a mainsail with two sets of reefing points and roller reefing genoa. Such rallies are a great way to learn and have fun in the company of experienced sailors.

Sailhead Flotation

Any flotation device at the top of the mast will obviously assist in avoiding an inversion after a capsize. Probably the neatest, and least to affect the normal wind pattern, is a pocket, sealable with a Velcro strip, sewn into the top of the mainsail, into which an airbag or piece of polystyrene can be fitted. Details of suppliers of the airbags can be obtained from the UKWA website.   An alternative to the sail-head flotation is the Secumar 'flotation cushion'. This works on the same principle as automatic life jackets. The main advantage is that it remains at the masthead even if the sail is reefed or removed. The disadvantages are its considerable cost and its additional weight at the top of the mast. This increases the heeling moment – possibly creating a capsize situation that might otherwise have been averted.

Wayfarers well snugged down in the Sea of Hebrides - note sailhead flotation device left

Capsizing

Capsize procedures are an element of sailing that ought to be practised at a very early stage. The standard RYA 'scoop' method is a useful system to adopt and should be practised. One person holds down or stands on the centreboard – minimizing any tendency to inversion. The crew meanwhile 'floats' in the helm area so that the boat is not pulled over. He can then throw over a righting line – a two-metre length of rope with holding loops tied in which should be permanently looped around the base of the shrouds. The crew can uncleat the mainsail and jib and pull in the spinnaker too. With the aid of the righting line the helm can gently ease the boat up so that it screws up into the wind and rights, scooping up the floating crew back into the boat. If anyone is still in the water, it is easiest to get in over the rear quarter by grabbing onto a toe-strap. The dished transom of the Mk IV should be a good entry point too. Providing everything in the boat is secured, or attached to it by a length of line, capsizing a Wayfarer should not be any great problem, but it is important to do everything possible to ensure it does not invert. In this case there can sometimes seem to be a vacuum holding the boat in the inverted position. To solve this get the crew to put his weight on one corner of the stern pushing it down into the water, this breaks the hold and makes it possible to get the boat back to the half-way position from where it is much easier to complete the righting process.

The other main issue is that when older marks of Wayfarer are righted, they come up full of water, which needs to be bailed out with a bucket, until the water is down to a level where the boat can be sailed, usually off the wind, to complete the emptying process through the self-bailers. This isn't an issue with the newer Wayfarer World or Mk IV designs, which will drain out quickly. It is useful to become sufficiently skilled to be able to climb over the side as the boat is capsizing, and climb back in again as it comes up, possibly without even getting wet! It is worth remembering though, that practice sessions are normally only done in relatively fine conditions. The procedure is more difficult in rough conditions at sea, with the waves and tide making the boat much more prone to an inversion. It is well worth also practising capsizing in rough sea conditions - and always under supervision, to ensure that no one ashore may mistake the situation for someone in distress and contact the Coastguard.

Small and easy additions to aid capsize recovery

The first is to fit righting lines as mentioned above. These consist of approximately two metre lengths of 8mm line secured to each shroud plate at one end, with a hand/foot-sized bowline loop at the other and figure of eight knots at intervals to stop hands from slipping along the rope. With these to hold onto, the crew can more easily right the boat. It is often suggested in the sailing books to use the jib sheets as righting lines, but this is not practical in the Wayfarer – dedicated righting lines are much better. Reasonably fit people can get back in the boat fairly easily, especially over the aft sections of the side-deck. But in more difficult conditions it is all too easy to become exhausted and/or hypothermic, making climbing back in impossible. So the second simple attachment is a length of rope with a loop in tied to the end to the thwart; this can be thrown over the side-deck to provide a foothold to make it easier to climb back in. The rolled gunwales on the Mk IV enable the possibility of hidden righting lines. Rope is taken from the port bridle position under the gunwale through a ring attached under the chain plate and then continues as elastic (bungee) around a ring under the bow and then back through another ring near the opposite chain plate where it again becomes rope that goes back to the starboard anchor point under the bridle fixing. The bungee keeps the line tight under the gunwale when not in use but allows it to extend out when needed. Small plastic ball stoppers can be fixed at the rope/bungee joins to limit the amount of line pulled through the rings when in use.

Practise capsizing in controlled conditions, with safety boat cover so that righting the boat in more difficult circumstances can be achieved more easily.

REEFING SYSTEMS

Cruising and day sailing should be about manageable boat handling and navigation. If the wind strength is increasing beyond the comfortable skill level of the helm and crew, then both sails should be reduced by reefing. Once the wind reaches force four and above, it can become too physically and mentally demanding to be constantly fine tuning the sails to cope with the stronger gusts. This increases the risk of capsize; a situation to be avoided at all costs without safety boat cover. It is essential to reef early and never wait to see if conditions improve - it is easier to shake out a reef than to put one in an increasingly strong wind. The choices for reefing are slab or roller reefing for the mainsail; and roller reefing the headsail or changing down to a smaller size. The golden rule for the mainsail is to keep the reefing system as simple as possible. It shouldn't take more than two minutes to complete a reef, and with practice it should be possible to get the time down to under a minute. It is advisable to set up a mainsail reefing system in such a way as to reduce the number of holes and fittings on the spars to a minimum, and worth taking care to ensure that holes for fittings are not initially drilled in the wrong place. Roller reefing the jib should be very fast – no more than a few seconds! There are a number of systems available to achieve this.

Slab versus Roller Reefing?

The predominant Wayfarer mainsail reefing system is slab reefing - sometimes referred to as jiffy reefing. It works without conflict with other systems on the boat, like the kicking-strap and centre-mainsheet. It will also work alongside a spinnaker pole stowed on the boom. The alternative system of roller reefing the mainsail around the boom is not suitable with a centre-mainsheet and requires the kicking strap to be removed and replaced with a makeshift strap rolled in with the sail. All this is not easy to do afloat in conditions when reefing is necessary; it takes far longer than slab reefing and the resultant sail shape is invariably very poor. The method does have some advocates, but because of the above concerns, only the slab reefing method is covered in this book.

Mainsail Reefing Points

Sail-makers will supply sails ready fitted with reefing points or they will convert an existing sail for you. For racers wishing to broaden their activities, an old racing sail is an ideal way of extending its useful life. There is much opinion about the height of the rows of reefing points above the boom. Many sail-makers tend to put the points a little too low. If the conditions are such that a reef is necessary, then it is worth taking out a reasonably large area of mainsail. A good benchmark is to have the points around one metre and two metres above the foot – the one metre reef points work well with the standard Wayfarer jib. It is advantageous to make the luff reefing points 100mm lower than those at the leech so that the boom rises slightly over the crew's heads. The second reefing point will come above the lowest batten and ideally this batten pocket should be re-aligned to run parallel to the rows of reefing points. Fit four small cringles along the sail for reefing ties for the first reef and three for the second. The simplest system for the reefing ties is to use 450mm lengths of shock-cord with 'Tyga Tie' shock-cord cleats on one side of the sail, and plastic ball stoppers on the other side to hold them in place.

Leech Reefing Lines

These should be of four to five mm diameter low stretch rope that is easy to grip in the hands. The leech reefing line needs to be anchored to the boom, passed up through the leech reefing cringle and back down to a block on the boom where it needs to pass forward to a cleat on the boom near the mast. The positions of the leech line anchor points and blocks on the boom needs to be found out by trial and error and depend on where the sailmaker fitted the reef cringles in the leech of the sail. One way to find out is by using adjustable Selden boom slides on the base of the boom to anchor the reef lines and as points to lash the blocks.

The images right show how boom track sliders can be used to trial reefing lines without the need to cut holes. Seen from the port side looking forwards the upper image shows the 1st reefing line on the right tied to a boom track slider. The 2nd reefing line can be seen passing forward via a block lashed to a boom slider. The lower image is the converse shown from starboard.

'Spree Lady' nicely balanced with a single reef in the mainsail and partially reefed genoa - using the Aero Luffspar system. The 450mm shock-cord ties with plastic ball stoppers for the second reef can be seen hanging down as can the modified batten pocket parallel to the boom.

The correct position is found when a reef is put in and the clew reefing cringle is found to be pulled both down and back, with the reefing line making an angle of about 45° between the sail cringle and the fittings on the boom. This keeps the foot of the sail taut to maintain a good shape. Once the positions are known a neat arrangement is to mount sheaves on the boom to lead the reefing lines forward inside the boom.

THE COMFORT AND SAFETY ZONE

In this more permanent arrangement the reefing lines are lead via sheaves into the boom to keep rope out of the way - but they can be led externally too.

Close up showing two reefs pulled in with the lines pulling the cringles down approximately 45 degrees.

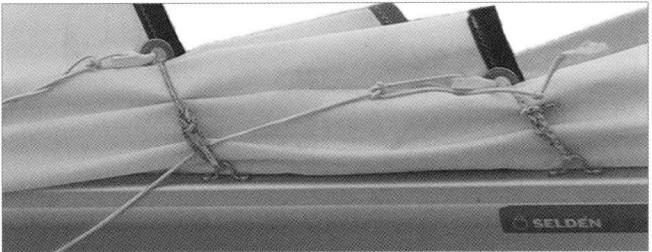

Fitting the reefing lines

The general arrangement of the lines is shown below: One end of the reefing line is secured - preferably spliced - to the boom slide or eye secured to the boom. The line is fed up through the first (or second) leech reefing cringle and then back down to the corresponding boom block (however fitted). If the lines are external they need to pass forward through loops (see images below left) or the spinnaker pole holder to stop them sagging when not in use.

The lines pass forward forward to a cleating arrangement near the mast – around 450mm from the gooseneck (see examples above right). These cleats should be situated on the boom such that the crew can carry out the reefing process standing entirely in front of the thwart.

General arrangement for two reefing lines with lines led inside the boom. Note the parallel batten.

Below: One reefing line emerging from the boom into a Clamcleat. The other line is on the other side. It is worth considering having them both emerging on the starboard side so they are easily accessible by the crew at the same time. A hook is shown to locate the luff reefing cringles, although not always user-friendly!

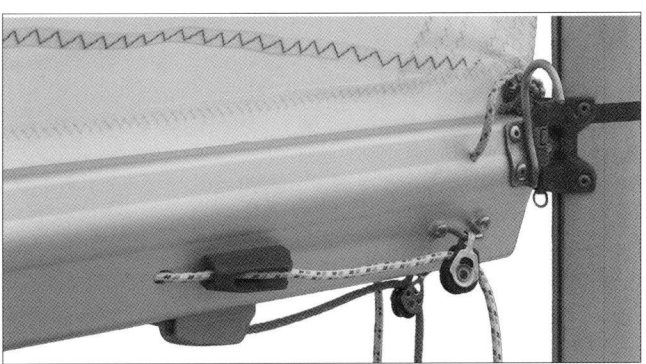

Another simple addition is the fitment of 'keepers' to the cleats below. These make cleating more secure and prevent unwanted cleating when a reef is being shaken out. Note also a bag to keep the reefing lines tidy. This example shows a single reefing line only.

Holding down the Tack

Various methods exist to secure the tack reefing line to the boom. It is possible to use the cunningham, if fitted, or a second reefing line to pull and fix the tack in place. Fittings for a luff reefing line can be fixed on the mast, rather than the boom, offering the advantage of a better angle of pull for the luff line and hence better tension along the foot of the sail. A slight disadvantage of this arrangement is the need to remember to release the luff line from the side entry cleat when lowering the sail. Another alternative fixing arrangement is to use a hook fitted onto the side of the boom, over which the luff reefing cringle is secured, (see image top right) or a 'cowhorn' fitting to replace the pivot bolt in the gooseneck. Both methods save using a length of line, but an open hook is not

a particularly user-friendly fitting for a small boat. The hook system on the side of the boom also has the disadvantage of exerting a pull on one side, resulting in a slight twist in the boom.

Another idea is to use a small stainless steel hook threaded onto the boom tack pin. The advantage is that the reef stays entirely on the boom, with no attachments needed to either the mast or the boom. For racers this is a means of fitting a system that is not permanent, especially when combined with using the sliders for the leech reefing lines, with only some sort of leech line cleating system needing to be put in place. Before deciding on a particular reefing system, have a good nose at what others have done – particularly at events like the annual Cruising Conference or a Wayfarer rally. Better to get it right first time!

GENOA FURLING DRUM SYSTEMS

A genoa furling system rolls the foresail around the luff wire to wrap it tidily out of the way once hoisted. This is used to prevent the sail flogging when launching, coming into land and anchoring - it keeps the jib quiet and out of the way. The system requires a furling drum (with top swivel) which should always be of the enclosed type and able to take sufficient 3mm thickness of line to completely furl a genoa - normally 16 to 18 turns. Recommended closed drum furling systems with stainless steel bearings are available from Harken, RWO, and Selden. The control line needs to be led back in such a way as to be simple for the crew - or helm if sailing single-handed - to cleat positively, so that there is no likelihood of the sail unfurling unintentionally. The jib halyard needs to have a standard tensioning device such as a cascade system, muscle box or highfield lever. There is a tendency for the forestay, if it has any slackness, to be wrapped into the genoa luff during the furling procedure, which quickly prevents any further furling of the foresail. Keeping the forestay tensioned parallel to the jib luff is essential, and it is best to fit some sort of spacer, like a plastic disc to fit over the upper part of the top swivel, (see image right). The best way to furl the sail is often to turn off the wind temporarily onto a near run - being careful not to gybe. This will blanket the genoa with the main, taking all the pressure out of the sail, which can then be quickly furled, before returning to the required course.

Although genoa furling is an extremely useful way of quickly tidying the foresail, sail makers do not generally recommend this method for racing sails, since it can slightly damage the sail material at the luff of the sail – as it is wound fairly tightly around the luff wire. Also, furling the genoa to reduce the size of the sail when sailing can only be used successfully in a very limited way, since if it is tried when sailing to windward any tension on the jib sheet will unwind the top of the genoa, and cause the top part of the sail to flog.

This is the Helyar flexible reefing spar system with a Harken furling drum.

GENOA REEFING SYSTEMS

A more complete solution is a full genoa reefing system: a tube, or reefing spar, is used either to replace or encase the jib luff wire. When the furling drum is turned, the top swivel, being directly connected, is also turned. This ensures that the sail is furled consistently along its length, and more importantly, when the sail is partially furled, any tension on the jib sheet will not unwind the top part of the sail. This enables the genoa to be reefed by any amount as required.

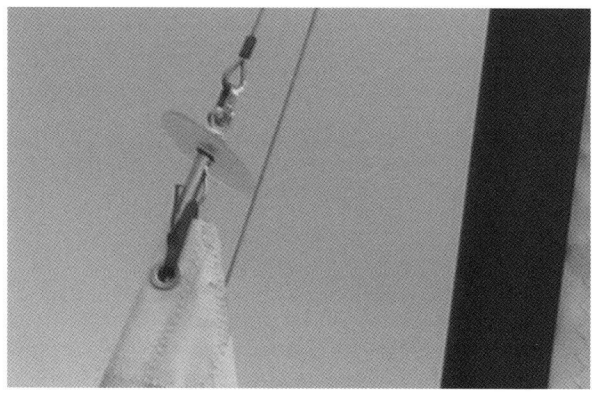

A plastic spacer keeps the forestay away from the top swivel

The diameter of the reefing spar can affect the flow of air over the leading edge of the genoa. It is advisable to fit extra sets of telltales on the genoa, further back from the luff, so that when the genoa is reefed, a set of telltales will still be visible to indicate the performance of the sail. The long reefing spar, with the genoa normally left permanently attached to it, can make the foresail less simple to transport, complicating the hoisting of the sail a little, and hence makes bridge shooting slightly less simple. For most experienced cruisers, however, the convenience of being

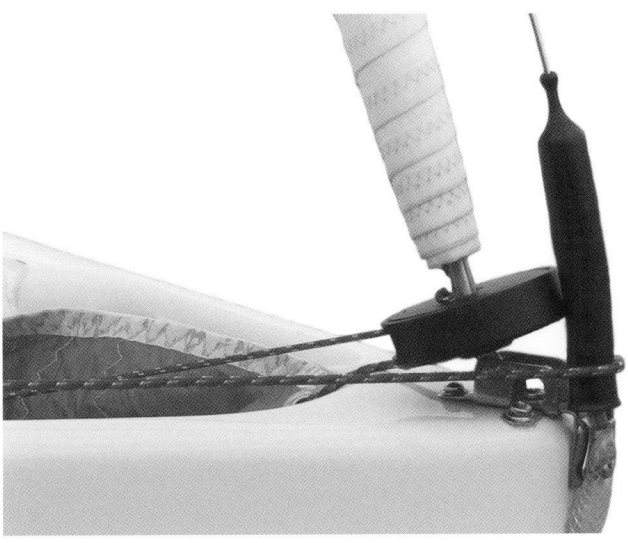

This Aero Luffspar genoa reefing system uses an integral spar/drum enabling the genoa to be set at near normal height over the deck. The slim spar is almost unnoticeable in use and therefore suitable for racing as well as cruising applications.

able to adjust the genoa to any size is regarded as being of far greater overall benefit than the slight disadvantages. There are a number of different makes and slightly varying systems currently available on the market, of which the following are popular:

Helyar Flexible Reefing Spars
This is probably the simplest and least expensive system, whilst still being extremely effective. It has the particular advantage for those who already have a good enclosed drum furling system of being able to incorporate this into the new reefing system, rather than making it redundant. The luff spar is made from a highly flexible 20mm diameter polypropylene type material and has the advantage of being simple to hoist and easily transportable - both the spar and the sail can be rolled along its length into a large circle, to be placed, say, inside the boat. The forestay can also be retained to provide normal mast support enabling the genoa and reefing spar to be removed with the mast still supported. www.flexible-reefing-spars.co.uk/

Aero Luff and Furling Spar
These are a new development in luff spars and made from carbon or glass fibre, with a carbon spiral outer binding to provide the spar with the torsional strength needed for the furling/reefing process. The spar is extremely lightweight and only 8mm in diameter. Since the thin spar is encased within the genoa luff sleeve, it provides the luff with a good aerofoil entry shape. The more basic 'Luff Spar 'system fits onto any existing furling drum and top swivel, and though it doesn't have the unlimited flexibility of the Helyar system, can be bent sufficiently to be passed under the spreaders to be laid back in the boat without detaching the spar from the furling drum. The 'Furling Spar' system incorporates its own furling drum and top swivel within the spar, with the furling drum set sufficiently low for there to be little difference in the height of the foot of the sail above the foredeck as compared to a normal sail, (see left), making it more suitable for racers and cruisers who prefer the convenience of furling the genoa away when not in use without compromising the sail's performance. www.aeroluffspars.co.uk/

Bartell
This is a highly sophisticated furling system with a correspondingly matching price, being two to three times the cost of the other systems. The reefing spar consists of a two-part aluminium aerofoil section, which is reduced to 20mm wide at its narrowest point. The sheathed wire running through the hollow centre of the reefing spar replaces both the forestay and halyard to provide support for the mast and this removes any possibility of a separate forestay snagging on the genoa as it is being reefed. http://bartels.eu/

HOW TO REEF
Reefing should always be carried out at the first sign of stronger wind conditions approaching, so it shouldn't need to be done as an urgent operation; although it is wise to have the skills to do so if an unexpected squall does arise. In this case, it is only necessary to secure the new tack and leech reefing points for the sail to be fully reefed. The excess sail may flap around untidily – but this can be rolled up and secured when a suitable opportunity permits. It is advisable to take the boat out on a quiet day and practise.

The normal regimen is for the helm to concentrate on sailing the boat, while the crew does the reefing. The reefing process is best done while continuing to sail on a reach, since the helm remains in control of the boat. If preferred, reefing can be carried out whilst hove-to if there is sufficient sea-room to allow for a few minutes of drifting. It is then advisable to furl or take down the genoa first as either backing this sail, or allowing it to flog, will increase the amount of drift during the reefing process.

The reefing process always starts by easing the kicker right off as far as it will go - or releasing it from the boom or mast in which case a simple clip-on system is recommended. Pull the leech reefing line so that the boom rises to the limit of the kicker travel, or until the first reefing point is reached if this is possible. Ease off the main halyard and lower sufficient sail to bring the boom horizontal again. (Care should be taken not to release the halyard completely thereby allowing the boom to drop down into the boat, or worse, the water). Repeat the process until the first reefing point is reached and cleat the reefing line. Release the main halyard further until the first reef luff cringle is level with the top of the boom and can be attached by means of a line or hook. Re-tension the main halyard as necessary, check the leech reefing line is completely tight and replace or tighten the kicker. The spare rope of the two reefing lines can be coiled and placed in the loose sail, which can be rolled or folded up along the boom, with the shock-cord ties being hooked up as far as the crew can reach in safety.

Taking out a reef

Taking out a reef is the reverse of the sequence described above, and can also be done whilst sailing. Release the sail ties; free off the kicker; release the luff reefing line and hoist the mainsail; secure the main halyard; release the leech reefing line; tighten the kicker. It will be noted that the reefing process – either putting one in or taking one out – is speeded up considerably by having a kicker arrangement that allows the boom considerable vertical travel.

Balancing the Rig

Sailing with a balanced rig is paramount and after reefing the mainsail, it is essential to reduce the area of foresail by a corresponding amount. It is therefore necessary to carry a jib, or have some sort of genoa reefing system as above. Should there be any doubts about the wind strength, it is more seamanlike to set off with a reefed main and reduced headsail. If the wind turns out to be light, it is less trouble to shake a reef out than to put a reef in later, should the wind increase. There is little merit in reducing the mainsail by more than two metres, as the ability to make to windward suffers. The boat is nicely balanced with one reef in the main and partially reefed genoa - or the genoa changed to a jib - in wind strengths of F4-5. Above F5, then two reefs in the main with the genoa area reduced to the size of a storm jib will enable a suitable crew to power the boat into the teeth of wind strengths in the region of F7. A Wayfarer also sails perfectly well on mainsail only; and when beating to windward in strong winds with no smaller foresail available than a genoa, it is better to sail without the genoa at all. The resulting lack of rig balance at least errs on the side of safety, as the boat will turn even more readily into the wind. This can be counteracted to some extent by raising the centreboard to half depth, which brings the centre of lateral resistance of the boat aft to better match the rig set-up. Tacking may be more difficult, as there is no foresail to back to help complete the manoeuvre. In this situation it is helpful to be able to sail backwards, as reversing the rudder will often help to complete the tack.

Sail balance is not at all critical when sailing off the wind and often apparently atrocious wind and sea conditions can be considerably calmed by taking down the mainsail, and sailing downwind on genoa or jib only. At wind strengths above a F6 it may be wise, particularly in difficult sea conditions, to consider dropping the main and run to safety under headsail. It is therefore always recommended when cruising to plan some downwind refuge run to should this become necessary. A Wayfarer also sails surprisingly well on genoa alone - less so on jib alone. It can even be made to go a bit to windward, but this can only be done by first gaining boat speed to provide some momentum, before gradually turning toward a close reach.

A reefed mainsail nicely balanced by a reefed genoa - in this case using the Helyar flexible luff spar

Summary of Reefing Procedure

- Reduce head-sail area to jib size or smaller.

- Sail on reach with complete control or heave-to ensuring there is sufficient sea room.

- Release or detach the kicker.

- Tension the leech reef line as far as the released kicker allows thus raising the boom – known as scandalising the sail.

- Release the main halyard and tension the luff reefing line or secure the luff reefing cringle - depending on system used.

- Re-tension the main halyard and check the leech reefing line is fully tensioned.

- Re-attach and/or tighten the kicker.

- Tidy excess reefing line tails and place in boom bag or the rolled up loose sail secured with shock-cord ties.

BUOYANCY TESTING

A Wayfarer must have an annual buoyancy test and endorsement in order to race at the class's Area, National, and International Championships. Additionally, such a test is a mandatory condition at many sailing clubs before members are permitted to sail in club events. Notwithstanding whether you are bound by such conditions; as a club racer, independent cruiser, or day sailor, the UKWA strongly recommends that a boat buoyancy check be carried out annually.

Marks 1 through to Mark III.
These Marks have front and particularly rear buoyancy tanks which often double up as stowage compartments for day sailors and cruisers. The large hatch covers providing access are particularly vulnerable to leakage – the seals and clamping mechanisms therefore need to be checked regularly. If this maintenance is neglected and the buoyancy areas fill with water it will not be possible to right the boat to continue sailing. The only possibility for saving the boat will be for it to be towed to the nearest shore, and since it will be almost impossible to keep the boat in an upright position; this is likely to result, at the very least, in a broken mast. The small circular inspection hatch covers, as well as the bungs, also need checking for water-tightness. It is every skipper's responsibility to ensure his or her boat is in a seaworthy state at all times.

Wayfarer World and the MK IV Wayfarers
These newer designs use dedicated buoyancy areas separate from stowage. There is much less routine maintenance – just the need to check the small circular inspection hatch covers and bungs for water-tightness.

The Dry Test

The usual method of buoyancy testing known as the 'dry' test measures the rate of loss of vacuum/pressure from each tank using a water-filled U-tube gauge made for example from 8mm bore clear plastic tubing. Air is blown into, or sucked from the tank to a prescribed pressure differential - 125mm or 5in of water - from the atmosphere. This level of pressure can also be produced by a low-pressure electric air pump of the type used for inflating airbeds - but pressure from an air compressor would be excessive and could damage the boat. The pressure differential must not fall to 50mm (2in) in less than 30 seconds. Clubs with Wayfarers often have a designated person who has this kit and can also sign buoyancy endorsements on the measurement certificate. But it is very useful to have your own test kit so that you can be sure of a pass before troubling the test person. Leaks can best be found by using the 'dry' test. Air can often be heard leaking from the offending points. Alternatively, brush a solution of washing-up liquid around the seals and joints in the tank, and watch for bubbles to appear to indicate the locations of a leak.

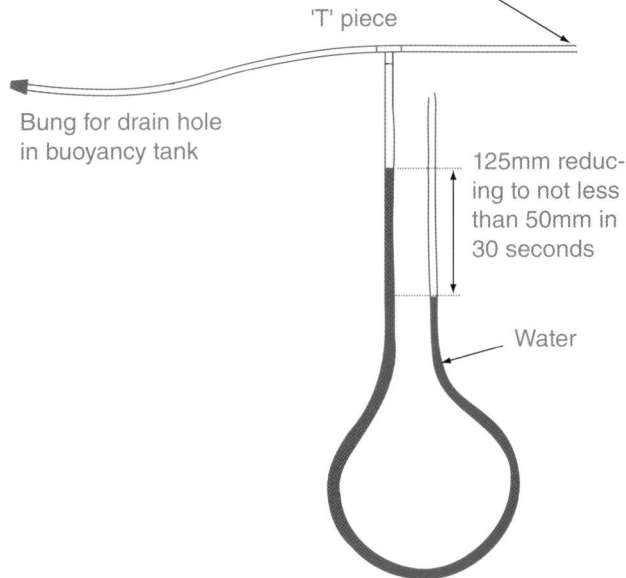

A 'Dry' buoyancy test kit made from plastic tubing

The Wet Test

Although not suitable for the Wayfarer World or Mark IV, the class rules allow the alternative less rigorous 'wet test' method for the earlier marks. The boat is capsized onto its side for five minutes with the helm and crew sitting on the side while the mast is held down by helpers. This is repeated for the other side - the boat not being bailed out in-between. The boat with crew still on board is brought upright and is required to float in its flooded state for a further ten minutes. After this time, the fore and aft tanks must be inspected and each must not contain more than 6.8 litres of water for the boat to pass. It can be a fun way to perform the test where there is a group of boats to be tested together so that there are sufficient helpers.

The criteria for both tests are listed in the Class Rules and must be witnessed by a UKWA Official Measurer or a Club Sailing Officer (e.g. Class Captain), who will endorse the Measurement Certificate. In the event of the boat failing either test, there is obviously a leak. The most common place for leaks in wooden boats is between the bulkheads and the deck. With GRP boats, the leaks are most commonly found along the gunwale, or beyond the bulkhead. Where leaks are through a join between the tank and the hull or deck, then the fibreglass joint will need to be examined to check that it has not become detached. If this is the problem, it will need to be repaired professionally. Minor leaks can be sealed with a proprietary sealant obtainable from chandlers. Bulkhead bungs may be made airtight by smearing them with Vaseline or the like. It is always advisable to have some way of making the bungs captive, as well as to carry a few as spares.

TROLLEYS, TRAILING, CARE AND MAINTENANCE

Boat Trolleys and Trailers

Boat trailers may seem an expensive item, but they provide the facility to take your Wayfarer to a wide variety of wonderful places. Whether for racing, cruising or family holidays this ability greatly enhances the enjoyment of Wayfarer sailing - not only in home waters, but internationally too. Where the boat is only sailed inland, a boat trailer on its own may be sufficient, since fresh water shouldn't corrode any well-greased bearings after launching. But the combination trolley/trailer is the handiest system for most applications. It provides the availability of a relatively lightweight trolley for easy launching and with the trolley's plastic wheel hubs is relatively impervious to seawater corrosion. The trolley part (with boat) is easily swung onto the trailer frame when needed, the trailer part (including hubs and brakes) not having to be used in seawater.

It is best to try before buying or alternatively get a recommendation. A well-balanced trolley/trailer should be very easy to use and is an excellent investment. When considering the purchase of a trailer, or combination trolley/trailer, check to see how easy it is to load and unload the boat. A jockey wheel fitted to the trolley will make the boat easier to launch and recover. One way of reducing any strain in loading a trolley onto a trailer – particularly for single-handed loading, is to fit a winch onto the front of the trolley. This winch can also be used to haul the trolley/trailer up a steep or slippery launching ramp. The handle at the front of the trolley or trailer needs to be at a comfortable pulling height, and it is worth ensuring everything about the trolley and trailer makes handling the boat ashore as easy as possible. It can be a false economy to buy the cheapest trolley/trailer system on the market – consider the overall ease of use of the design.

Whatever type of trailer system is used, it must be strongly built, since the Wayfarer is a relatively heavy dinghy - *the boat should rest on the trolley or trailer with all the weight on the keel – being the strongest part of the hull – with a small gap between the bilge runners and any support, enabling the boat to rock very slightly from side to side.*

There is a small amount of routine maintenance - keep the wheel bearings greased and check that the tyre pressures are at the recommended settings before each trip. The trolley tyres should not be over-inflated as they can be vulnerable to bursting in strong sunshine – somewhere in the 20-25 lb range works satisfactorily.

Combination Trolley-trailer

#	Item	#	Item
1	Cross bar and straps	7	Mast & lighting board support using rudder gudgeon & pintle
2	Front mast support	8	Jockey wheel
3	Under cover (optional)	9	Trailing top cover - reduces wind turbulence and drag & helps improve fuel consumption. Also keeps gear relatively secure and out of sight.
4	Spare wheel	10	Safety strap
5	Trolley wheel	11	Towing socket
6	Lighting board	12	Lighting connector

Road Towing

It is important to make sure that the boat is properly secured to the trailer, though care needs to be taken not to over-tighten any ratchet-type straps, causing possible distortion to the hull. If unsupported along its length, the mast is best secured by laying the track uppermost, with the base of the mast at the stern of the boat. It is advisable to make up a support for the centre of the mast, which can be temporarily fitted into the tabernacle. This will prevent the mast from flexing during transportation, and allow the mast to be transported whichever way up is most convenient. It is inadvisable to carry heavy items like outboards in the boat whilst towing, since the extra weight could not only damage the boat, particularly when loaded at the stern where there is no trailer support, but could also put the trailer load above the safe towing weight for the vehicle you are driving. It would be unusual for a Wayfarer owner to be stopped and directed to take their vehicle and trailer to a weighbridge to be weighed, but it is possible to be fined for each axle that is overweight. In order to ensure that a trailer does not unnecessarily attract a police officer's attention, it would be worth making sure of the following legal requirements:

1. The boat is properly loaded and secured.
2. The lighting board is fully operational.
3. The tyres are correctly inflated, with the tread above the legal limit and not mixed cross-ply and radial.
4. There is a locking device for the lifting handle.
5. A safety line or chain is fitted between the car and trailer.
6. All unbraked trailers have to have a manufacturer's plate mounted on the nearside of the towbar giving the unladen and maximum permitted weights and the year of manufacture.

Other general points on towing:

1. A full licence must be held to tow a trailer, and anyone who has passed a driving test after July 1996 is not allowed to tow any sort of trailer without passing a separate 'towing test'.
2. Your insurance company should be informed that you intend to use your car for towing a trailer.
3. The maximum speed limit for towing is 60 mph on motorways and dual carriageways, and 50 mph on other derestricted roads.
4. A trailer may not be towed in the outside lane of motorways with three or more lanes – except where roadworks or passing abnormal loads dictate.
5 The overhang of the mast at the rear of the boat should not exceed 1.08 metres. Where it does exceed this amount, it needs to be marked - though it is always worth marking the end of any protruding mast.
6. Always carry a spare wheel, and check the wheel bearings are not worn and are well greased before setting out.

Boat Covers

Boat covers are generally made from PVC or polycotton. Canvas covers are more expensive but are essential for wood or composite boats, as the fabric allows the boat to 'breathe' and thus reduces the humidity inside the covered area. PVC is quite adequate for GRP boats. Sunlight will eventually cause the material of PVC covers to break down; and continual wetness will rot the fabric of canvas. Care must be taken not to leave a PVC cover touching the gelcoat of glass fibre boats for a long period of time, since it causes the gelcoat to become detached from the glass fibre, which results in 'bubbles' appearing on the surface. It is best to let the boat drain freely to keep moisture levels low. An over-boom cover is the most popular type, since it will shed the rain well - providing the sides are tied down securely. It is useful to have a cover which completely covers the transom on wooden boats to minimise sun erosion of the varnish.

General Maintenance
Weekly

Boats sailed regularly at sea need to be hosed down well with fresh water to prevent corrosion, paying particular attention to the metal fittings and running gear such as cleats and turning blocks. The clips should be released from all hatch covers at the end of each sail in order to take the pressure off the rubber seal. When the hatch cover is left clipped down, the rim will form a permanent indentation in the rubber, making the seal less effective.

Yearly

It is important that the front and rear buoyancy compartments are watertight and this should be tested at least annually - see the 'Buoyancy Testing' in Chapter 5. Check the rubber seals on the hatch covers first, and replace them if the seal has any permanent indentation, or appears in a generally poor state. Hatch clips may need adjusting to secure the hatch covers tightly. There are specialist Wayfarer suppliers who stock the rubber seals used for the hatches of the older marks of Wayfarer. These can be glued in position using a strong impact adhesive. The ends can be butt jointed along the middle of the front or back section, and a small mitre can be carefully cut half way through at each corner to keep the corners flat. However, it is best to cut out too little, rather than too much (it is useful to practise on the old rubber seal), and if not confident about achieving a perfect join, then it is probably better just to bend the seal around the corner.

Every fitting on the boat should be thoroughly inspected before the start of each sailing season (as well as before any major sea sailing trips) and any items at all suspect should be repaired or replaced. All screws should be tightened, and whenever this results in the head turning continuously, measures should be taken to ensure the screw has a firm hold. (This can be done by removing the screw and either filling the hole with epoxy or, if into wood, by gluing in a round plug of (preferably) hardwood – in both cases the screw hole area must be perfectly dry).

The shrouds should be carefully inspected, particularly where the eye splices have been swaged at the ends, and replaced if in a poor state. The shrouds should always be replaced if one of the wire strands is found to be broken, (normally checked by running the finger and thumb lightly along the wire), for it is likely that other strands are also weak and may break at a critical time. It is far easier to re-do these as part of the winter maintenance schedule, than at some inopportune moment when rigging the boat, or even more critically, for a shroud to fail whilst sailing the boat.

Wooden boats need to be checked thoroughly for any 'soft' areas, being a sign the wood is starting to rot. This is particularly likely in areas of the lowest parts of the buoyancy tanks or beneath the floorboards, where a residual amount of water may have been left unnoticed for much of the sailing season. Centreboard housings are particularly prone to this. Minimal damage can usually be repaired using an epoxy resin, but in extreme cases, there may be a need for the whole centreboard housing to be replaced completely. Be aware if this major repair is necessary, that the UKWA needs to be notified before any work is started, (should a measurement certificate be required after completion). GRP boats can usually be repaired without too much difficulty.

Removing the Centreboard

The centreboard is most easily removed with the boat on its side. This can best be done with the hull lying on an area of soft ground or old mattresses with the mast up. Leverage can then be applied to the mast to pull the boat over, with a weight being placed on the top of the mast to keep it in this position. The process can also be carried out on a boat trolley by pulling the trolley forward relative to the boat, so that the trolley axle clears the centreboard housing. The stern of the boat will need to be lifted, and supported on a suitable trestle to allow the centreboard to be lowered. The centreboard can then be gently eased out, raising the stern as necessary to allow it to clear the housing. Lining up the bolt holes when re-fitting the centreboard back into the boat is most easily done by drawing lines on the centreboard which radiate from the bolt hole, once a line has been located by looking through the centreboard case, movement along the line will locate the hole. This exercise is best done when the centreboard is fitted into the case in the 'fully up' position.

Storage

It is advisable to store a wooden boat under cover during the winter. If this is not possible, then the cover should be completely waterproof whilst still allowing air to circulate freely beneath it, so that the inside of the boat does not remain damp. Always raise the bow of a wooden boat (on its trolley) onto a trestle or similar, so that any condensation or rainwater collecting in the hull drains towards the stern tank. Water collecting at the bulkheads can penetrate the varnish and cause rot in the wood. In this case, repair to the bow bulkhead is much more serious than a repair to the stern tank. A GRP boat can be left out over winter (preferably in a frost-free area) without a cover. It is however recommended that the boat is turned upside down and well supported by trestles with no significant overhang, so that there is no stress at any particular point. Hatch covers should be loosened, and if plastic sheeting is used to offer some protection, it should not be left touching the gelcoat surface.

Wooden Boat Maintenance

It is not within the scope of this book to cover repairs in detail. There are many books that give advice on this specialist subject. Any varnishing or painting should be done in a dust-free environment, with successive coats either applied before rubbing down becomes necessary, or after rubbing down with a fine grade of wet and dry. To bring a wooden hull to its optimum condition, it is best to carefully strip off all the old paint, and make good any holes or damage. It is likely that all the screw holes have been filled with a chalk based filler. All traces of this material need to be removed, and the spaces refilled with epoxy filler*. The hull then needs priming with at least two coats of epoxy primer before finishing with either a traditional polyurethane coat, or a two-pack epoxy coating. The initial cost of the two-pack epoxy is high, but can be justified by it having at least a 10-year life span - if the surface is not damaged - together with a much higher resistance to abrasion damage. Top racers take considerable care to make sure the hull and overall boat weight is down to the minimum allowed, and that the underwater section is as perfectly smooth and fair as is possible to achieve.

* This is essential to avoid the outlines of screw holes reappearing in the topcoat as the integrity of your new epoxy primer is breached!

Repairs to GRP Boats

Any damage to the gelcoat surface of a GRP hull will allow water to ingress into the glass fibre matting, not only ultimately weakening its structure, but also increasing the hull's overall weight. Glass fibre repairs are not difficult to carry out, but anyone with no previous experience of working in this material would be advised to have a knowledgeable assistant for any first repair work. Working in glass fibre is generally messy, and the material can also cause skin and lung problems. It is therefore recommended that a barrier cream or thin plastic gloves are used to protect the hands, and a dust mask is worn whenever the repair work causes glass fibre dust to be present in the air. Glass fibre work is best carried out in a warm, dry atmosphere. Serious damage repair of GRP boats is best not attempted without considerable experience and the correct tools and conditions, as stresses can be set up in the laminates, which could weaken the integrity of the hull.

Often the surface of the gelcoat becomes chipped, scratched or discoloured. Places where the gelcoat has been chipped away to expose the glass fibre beneath should be repaired as soon as possible to prevent the water saturating the glass fibre. Where this has already occurred, the surface should be thoroughly dried before a gelcoat covering is applied. Most chandlers stock (white) gelcoat repair kits, though a coloured hull presents more of a problem. It is possible that the builder may be able to provide a reasonably matching colour. When applying gelcoat to the repair, it should be coated above the level of the surrounding area – sellotape can then be applied over the repair to contain the gelcoat and give it a uniform thickness. The excess gelcoat is best removed by carefully slicing it through with a razor blade shortly after it has set, but before it has reached its full hardness. Scratches and crazing can be scoured along their length with a sharp edge, cleaned with acetone, and filled with gelcoat. Whilst an expert produces results that make it difficult to see the repair, it is far less easy for an unskilled person to produce the same results. Any scratches and crazing which have not penetrated through the glass fibre can often be improved by just polishing the area with a proprietary gelcoat cleaner, particularly one containing oxalic acid. Discolouration is also best dealt with by polishing with a proprietary cleaner.

Special paints are available for glass fibre boats, but are expensive, add weight, and may well de-value the boat to a discerning buyer, since such a person will be concerned about what damage the painted surface might be concealing. The boat has to be prepared very thoroughly, which will take a considerable amount of time, as will the application of the paint. It is therefore worth carefully considering whether re-painting is actually worthwhile. An alternative solution might be to sail the boat for a few seasons, learning where the various fittings are best suited for the type of sailing being undertaken, and then sell the boat on, replacing it with a newer boat in better condition. This is likely to cost little or no more than re-painting an older GRP Wayfarer – and will save an infinite amount of time.

Foils

The importance of an ultra-smooth surface applies even more to the foils than the hull. The centreboard works with lateral pressure to minimise leeway. It has been calculated that compared with the hull, the centreboard is working at four times the hydrostatic pressure, and will therefore create four times the drag unless perfectly smooth. Timber-laminated epoxy sheathed centreboards and rudders are generally recommended over the standard shatterproof ply versions commonly found on older boats – though the latter have largely been superseded by moulded GRP versions for new boats. If properly finished, a ply centreboard or rudder is perfectly adequate for all but the most discerning helmsmen. Centreboard and rudder foils can be between 19mm and 21mm thick. Annual checks of the foils should be made for any surface damage, as well as any delamination of ply boards, particularly where the centreboard works against the bottom of the housing, and the area of rudder between the jaws of the stock. The foils will need replacing/repair if any deterioration is found. It is imperative that the outer shape of the centreboard and rudder conform to the official drawings. The specification requires a tolerance of only +0mm to -6mm, and it is quite usual for this to be specifically checked at an Area, National or World Championship meeting. Some of the foil's efficiency, particularly with regard to the centreboard, will be lost if it is ground away at the tip. If you normally sail in an area with shallow water it would be well worth fitting brass tips to both foils before they are painted. The more expensive foils have an additional area of epoxy coating around the tip to afford some protection, but touching the sea bottom should be avoided at all costs. The leading and trailing edges of the foils need to be accurately profiled (centreboard max 64mm, rudder max 50mm) - this is another area that is checked during scrutinizing.

To produce a final perfect finish on foils, they should be primed with at least 2 coats of epoxy primer, followed by several coats of undercoat, smoothing down any imperfections between every second coat. After allowing this to harden for at least a week, the surface will need to be rubbed perfectly smooth and flat with wetted 320-grade Silicone Carbide (Wet and Dry) paper. This needs to be followed with 2 to 4 coats of two pack polyurethane enamel, again allowing plenty of time to cure before rubbing down with wetted 600-grade paper. It is then finally burnished with wetted 1200-grade. This will provide a championship quality board, which feels as smooth as the finest silk, and looks almost opaque. Having taken so much trouble to achieve foils with a perfect finish, it is worth remembering the time spent on them when approaching the shore or during launching! It is recommended that the rudder be kept in a padded bag for transportation. For those who prefer a somewhat easier way of achieving the above, the Wayfarer boat builders, as well as a number of specialist foil manufacturers, are able to supply fully finished foils in wood/epoxy or GRP.

Spars

The mast and boom should be washed thoroughly in fresh water at the end of the season, checking particularly to see if there is any corrosion between the aluminium spars and any fittings. Stainless steel screws, bolts and rivets in contact with aluminium are subject to electrolytic corrosion in the presence of salt, making them difficult if not impossible to remove after just one season or two. This can be prevented by applying 'Duralac' sealant paste and jointing compound - obtainable from good chandlers - before securing any spar fitting with stainless steel screws or rivets. Again the stainless steel shroud plates and fittings should not be wrapped around the mast during winter storage, as the contact points on the mast will corrode, especially if left damp and salty. Mast bags are very convenient for keeping the rigging tidy while trailing, but they should be removed to allow ventilation for winter storage. If stored horizontally over the winter, masts should be supported at sufficient points along their length to maintain their true alignment.

Sails

The main should be rolled from the head, in line with the battens and then kept rolled with a sail tie. As you roll up the sail parallel to the battens, keep the material crease-free. Be very careful not to pull out any folds or pleats by pulling them along the tube you create as this damages the sailcloth. If creases occur, just unroll the sail slightly and shake out or push out the fold from underneath. If the angle of the bottom batten pocket has been changed to accommodate a reefing point, then this batten is best removed. The foresail should be rolled carefully along the line of the luff wire, starting at the head and keeping the sailcloth nice and even - use a sail tie to stop it springing open. This is best done by leaving the tack shackled on and the jib sheet pulled in reasonably tight. The sail can then be rolled around the luff wire. Alternatively lay the genoa across the boat with the head to windward and roll it again starting from the head to the foot along the luff wire. The spinnaker should be flaked and then folded carefully into its bag after use. It is best not to leave it in the chute for any length of time - especially with load on the patch. The sail should not be dried by hoisting and letting it flap as this stretches the edges. Sails are easiest to furl with two people – one at each end of the roll. Each crew should stop what they are doing without waiting to be asked and assist if the other starts to furl a sail – it saves time and makes a better job.

Stains are best removed as soon as possible. There are a number of specialist solutions to treat various types of stain, but generally washing up liquid (very safe!) or acetone (highly inflammable and should be used outdoors to avoid breathing in any vapour) will remove the worst of most marks. Acetone will also remove the old glue if changing sail numbers on a mainsail.

Halyards
All halyards should be checked thoroughly, particularly the genoa halyard, where it is advisable to look for any wear in the rope tail at the point it is spliced onto the wire, or broken strands around the swaged ferrule on the lower wire loop, as well as along the length of the wire itself.

Ropes
Ropes (particularly the main and genoa sheets) can be washed very effectively in a washing machine with normal washing detergent. This will remove any salt accumulation over the sailing season, and give a much better 'feel' to them for future use. A warm water programme for synthetics will prevent the ropes from shrinking, and the agitation in the machine will help dislodge any grit that often accumulates in them.

Floorboards
The separate floorboards fitted to earlier marks of boat are best painted with non-slip deck paint. A cheaper alternative is to use ordinary paint or varnish sprinkled with granulated sugar or sand, thoroughly washing the surface after the paint or varnish has dried.

Self-Bailers
It is worth checking that there is no sand or grit in the rubber seal of the self-bailers, and testing that they don't leak (by pouring water into the self-bailer area of the boat, and checking to see if any drips appear under the hull). Being fully watertight may only be of some importance to those who cruise and sleep in the boat, but if water tightness is a criterion, then it might be worth trying to ensure a good seal in a leaking self-bailer with silicone sealant. Vaseline will need to be applied to all areas where a permanent bond is not required – including the rubber seal – before applying the silicone to the (closing) face of the bailer, and clamping the bailer shut.

Buying Second-Hand
The copyright holder issues sail numbers for each licensed boat built. When purchasing a second-hand Wayfarer, prospective buyers should ensure that their intended purchase has a licence plate with the boat's sail number - normally fixed to the sloping part of the centreboard case. For wooden boats, the sail number is engraved on the inside of the transom.

Where no licence plate exists, a new one, (with a prefix 0 number) will only be issued after exhaustive enquiries into the boat's background to ensure that it is a genuine Wayfarer, this process being carried out via the Class Association.

The Wayfarer is a very solid boat, and can take a great deal of punishment before it is beyond repair. Many older second-hand boats have crazing on the gel coat in various areas, indicating they have been well used. This is generally only superficial damage, and does not usually affect the integrity or seaworthiness of the boat. Of much greater concern would be major repairs to any part of the boat, particularly those caused by an obvious collision.

It is important to note that damage to a Wayfarer can occur if the launching trolley has at some stage persistently taken the boat's full weight on the two bilge keels rather than the main keel; this can be easily seen as a distortion to the underwater shape and causes the floor bearers to come away from the inner hull. It is therefore advisable to remove the floorboards to check the floor bearers before buying. The hull should always have been supported along its central keel, and should slightly rock from side to side on its bilge keel trolley supports – see Boat Trolleys and Trailers above.

TABLE 4. Mast Set-up Procedure

Tools Required	Long tape measure, rig tension gauge. For more details - see Pages 12-14	
Boat Equipment	Adjustable spreaders, adjustable mast step, jib halyard tensioning device.	
1	With mast flat on floor, set up the spreader deflection (200mm) and length measurements (508mm). Make sure that the spreader angle is the same each side.	
2	Stand the mast in the boat with the shrouds in position. The mast should be hard up against the mast aft heel pin but without the mast pivot pin in position.	
3	Put the jib up and pull on the jib tension - 150kg. Check this with the rig tension gauge.	
4	Hoist the tape measure up to the top of the mast until 5867mm (19' 3") comes to the top of the gooseneck band. Fix the halyard at this point.	
5	Swing the tape measure aft to the back of the boat. For Mark IVs measure to the top of the transom; range 7240mm - 7290mm (23' 9" - 23' 11"). For earlier marks take the reading at the underside of the mainsheet track. The range is 7135mm - 7190mm (23' 5" - 23' 7").	
6	If the measurement is correct go to step 9.	
7	Rake too much? Move the pins in the shroud adjusters up.	Rake too little? Move the pins in the shroud adjusters down.
8	Go back to step 3 and repeat the steps until the required measurement is reached. The rig tension will have to be eased each time the shroud adjusters are altered.	
9	Does the pivot pin fit through the hole without touching the sides? If yes go to step 11.	
10	Does pin jam against the front of mast? Move the mast step pin backwards.	Does pin jam against the back of mast? Move the mast step pin forwards.
11	The last thing to check is the mast bend. Pull the main halyard tight against the mast at the gooseneck and measure from the back of the mast to the halyard at spreader height. The normal range is between 25mm and 38mm.	
12	If too little bend adjust the spreaders backwards a small amount.	If too much bend, adjust the spreaders forwards a small amount.
13	After adjusting the spreaders go back to step 2 and check the measurements again.	

INDEX

Aerofoil Section 5, 6
Anchor & Chain 12, 55, 58, 61
    CQR 55, 61
    Danforth 55, 61
    Drum 61
    Grapnel 55
Annual
    Buoyancy Test 81
    Checks 84 - 87
Asymmetric Spinnaker
    and pole 4, 15, 19
Auto-Release Cleat 6

Barber Hauler/
    Twinning Lines 5, 16, 17, 30
Battens 8, 25, 26, 44
Beach Landing / Rollers 62
Beating (The Beat) 36, 46, 50
Boat Checks 34, 45, 55, 58, 84-87
Boat Speed 36
Boat/Boom Tents 58, 64, 65
Boat Covers 84
Boom 5, 25, 26, 38, 39, 44, 48
    Maintenance 86
    Sections 7
    Underside Track 7
Bridle 5, 11, 24
    Fixed/Adjustable 25, 26
Bridge Shooting 62
Buoyancy
    Buoyancy Hatches 55, 84
    Watertight /
    Compartments / Tanks 2, 3, 84
    Integrity 3
    Test - Wet and Dry 4, 81

Capsize 21, 27, 75
Cascade System 9
    Genoa Halyard 9, 10, 12
    Kicking Strap 9
Centreboard 22, 26, 28, 38, 39, 40,
    44, 61
    Angle of Leading Edge 5
    Brass strip 6
    Friction Grip 6
    Maintenance 86
    Packing Strips 6
    Penetration beneath Keel 6
    Pivot Bolt 6
    Removing 85
    Slot Gaskets 6

Charts 56, 58
Chines 5
Class Measurer 4
Clear Air/Wind 36, 39
Clothing 45, 73
Coastal 53
Coastguard 56
Compass 10, 12, 58
Composite 3
Cooking Stoves 65
Crewing 45
Cruising Attributes 2, 3
Cruising Conference 53
Cruising Logs/ Library 57, 58
Cruising Rallies 53
Cruising Trophies 57
Cruise to Blackwater Rally 67
Cruise - Sound of Jura 69
Cunningham 8, 10, 11, 24 ,25, 29, 38
    Tension Setting Guide 14

Day Sailing 9, 19
Dimensions 1
Dri-bags 2, 4, 58
Dry Suits 73

Estuary 53
Experience Guide
    Inland Sailing 54
    Estuary Sailing 54
    Sea Sailing 54
    Advanced Open Sea 54

Fenders 58, 62
First-aid Kit 58
Flares 57, 58
Foam-sandwich 3, 4, 21
Fore and Aft Trim 26
Foredeck 5, 12
Foresails 9
Forestay 5, 7, 9, 22, 28, 62

Genoa 8, 9, 22, 26, 58, 75
    Clew 8
    Fairlead & Track 9, 10
    Furling Gear 22, 53, 79
    Halyard 7, 10, 13, 23
    Leech 5, 23
    Luff 5, 8, 9, 22
    Luff cunningham 39
    Reefing System 53, 58, 78-80
    Setting Guide 14
    Sheets 9, 10, 23, 27, 58
    Window 8

Gooseneck 5, 11, 12, 16
GPS 56, 57
Gudgeons/Pintles 5
Gusts 26, 38, 44
Gybe/Gybing 11, 27, 29, 30, 31, 33,
    44, 48, 50, 60, 75
Gybe Mark 27, 30, 38, 39, 51

Hatch covers 2
Heave-to 22
Heeling 22, 26, 28, 36, 44
Highfield Lever 9, 10, 12
Hull 22

Inland 53
Inspection Hatch 10
International Rally 53
International Rules for Prevention
    of Collisions at Sea 56

Kicking Strap 5, 9, 10, 13, 24, 25, 26,
    29, 35, 36, 38, 39, 44, 48
Kicking Strap
    Tension Setting Guide 14

Jib 8,9
Jib Sheet 5
Jib Sheet Tension Setting Guide 14

Keel Bands 5

Launch Site Directory 53
Lay Lines 38
Leeward Mark 39, 51
Leeway 5, 25, 29
Lifelines 57

Mainsail 8, 58
    Backwinding 23
    Boat Number 8
    Clew 8
    Clew Outhaul 10, 11, 24, 25, 38
    Foot 8
    Foot Tension Setting Guide 14
    Halyard 10, 12, 24
    Head 8
    Leech 5, 8, 22, 25, 26, 40, 48
    Sailmaker's Logo 8
    Setting Guide 14
    Window 8

Mainsheet 5, 25, 26
    Block, Ratchet Block 5, 11
    Centre Sheeting 11
    Tension 39, 48
    Tension Setting Guide 14
    Track 11
    Transom Sheeting 11

Maintenance 84, 85, 86, 87

Mast
    Chocks 12-13, 24-25
    Chock/Ram Setting Guide 14
    Foot Position/Track 12, 13
    Heel 13
    Limit Pin 13
    Maintenance 86
    Pivot Pin 10, 12, 13
    Pivot Hole 12
    Pre-bend 13-14, 24-25
    Rake 12, 40
    Ram 5, 12-14, 24-25
    Selden E Section 7
    Setup 12-14, 88
    Sheaves 7, 13, 16
    Spreaders 7

Masthead Buoyancy 8, 56, 74
Masthead Light 57
Measurement Certificate 4
Muscle Box 9, 12

Oars 56, 59, 63
One-Design Principle 2, 48
Open Sea 53
Outboard Motor 56, 57, 60
    Brackets 60
    Storage 61
    Steering 61
    Buying 61

Paddling 60, 63
Penalty Turns 42
Personal Buoyancy 55, 73
Pointing 37, 48
Port Tack 37
Portsmouth Yardstick 1
Protected/semi/unprotected
    cruising areas 53
Protesting & Alternative
    Procedures 42
Pumps 59

Qualifications Day/Coastal Skipper/
    Yachtmaster Offshore 56

Racing Rules of Sailing 48
Radar Reflector 57
Ratchet Blocks 9, 10
Reaching 28, 29, 38, 44
Reefing Points 8
Reefing Systems 75-80
Rig Balance 5, 9, 13, 80
Rig Tension 12, 24, 37, 39
Rig Tension Gauge 12
Rig Tension Setting Guide 14
Roll Tacking 27
Roller Reefing 76
Rowing 59
Rowlocks 59
Rudder 5, 6, 22, 35, 39, 58
    Stock 5, 6
    Blade (lifting) 5, 6
    Long Blade 6
Running 39, 44, 51

Safety Boats 53
Sail Limit Bands
    "Black Bands" 4, 9, 12
Sailhead Flotation Device 56, 74
Sailing Instructions 34, 46
Sea Breeze 40, 41
Second-hand 2, 4, 87
Self-build Kits 2
Self-bailers 3, 4, 5, 58
Self-draining 3
Self-inflating Life Jackets 73
Sheaves 7
Shrouds 5, 7, 13
Shroud Adjusters 5, 7, 10, 13, 24
Sitting Out 46
Slab Reefing 53, 76
Sleeping Aboard 66
Slot Gaskets 5,6
Solo/Single-handed Sailing 53
Spares 58
Spinnaker 8, 10, 15, 28, 44, 50
    Chute 4, 17, 18, 28
    'D' Ring on Mast 16,17
    Guy 16, 17, 28, 29
    Halyard 7, 17, 28, 30, 31
    Hoisting/Launching 18, 30, 44, 51
    Leeward/Windward Hoist 28
    Piston Hooks & Release Cord
        15, 16
    Pole 5, 15, 17, 28, 31, 44
    Pole Downhaul 16, 17
    Pole Uphaul 10, 13, 16, 17, 28, 30
    Ramp 15, 16

Spinnaker (continued)
    Reaching Hook 17
    Sheets 5, 10, 15-17, 28-30
    Trimming 28
    Twin Pole System 18

Spreaders 7
    Adjusters 7
    Length, Angle, Span 12

Starboard Tack 37, 50
Starting 33, 35, 41, 45-47, 50
Storage 85
Stowage 2, 4, 58
Structural Changes 4

Tabernacle 5, 12, 61
Tack/Tacking 11, 27, 33, 36, 38, 46,
    47, 50
Telltales 8, 23, 26, 36
Thwart 5
Tidal Current/Flow 37, 38, 46, 53
Tidal Training 53
Tide Tables 56
Tiller 5, 6, 22, 58
    Extension 5, 6
Toestraps 5, 10, 11
Towing 61
Towpath Hauling 64
Trailing/ Road Towing 83, 84
Transom 11, 13, 60
Transom Flaps 4, 5
Traveller Rail 12

United Kingdom Wayfarer Assn. 1

VHF 57

Waves 38, 39, 44
Wayfarer
    Class Rules 2, 12, 13
    GRP 2, 3
    Insignia 8
    International Committee 1
    Types 2, 3, 4, 21
    Wood 2
Weather Forecasts 40, 41, 56
Weather Helm 26, 37, 40
Wet Suits 73
Winds/Airs
    Light 25, 26, 31, 36, 50
    Medium 24, 44
    Strong 25, 27, 29, 44, 49
Wind Bend 36, 49
Wind Shifts 36
Windward Mark 38, 49, 50